201
Killer Cover Letters

Sandra Podesta

Andrea Paxton

McGraw-Hill

New York   San Francisco   Washington, D.C.   Auckland   Bogotá
Caracas   Lisbon   London   Madrid   Mexico City   Milan
Montreal   New Delhi   San Juan   Singapore
Sydney   Tokyo   Toronto

Library of Congress Cataloging-in-Publication Data

Podesta, Sandra.
    201 killer cover letters / Sandra Podesta, Andrea Paxton.
        p.   cm.
    Includes index.
    ISBN 0-07-050456-3 (pbk.)
    1. Cover letters.   2. Applications for positions.   3. Job hunting.
    I. Paxton, Andrea.   II. Title.
    HF5383.P63   1995
    808'.06665—dc20   95–37325
                                                                        CIP

McGraw-Hill

A Division of The McGraw·Hill Companies

        6 7 8 9 10   FGRFGR   9 9 8

PN 0-07-050457-1
PART OF
ISBN 0-07-050456-3

The sponsoring editor for this book was Betsy Brown, the assistant editor was Danielle Munley, the editing supervisor was Fred Dahl, and the production supervisor was Suzanne Rapcavage. It was set in Palatino by Inkwell Publishing Services.

Contents

Introduction   *v*

How to Use This Book and Disk   *ix*

1. The Top Ten Rules for Writing Killer Cover Letters   *1*
The Basic Do's and Don'ts for Cover Letters
and All Your Jobhunting Correspondence

2. How to Identify and Sell Your Strengths   *12*
How to Identify Your Unique Skills and Talents and
What They Offer Your Next Employer —
Worksheets 2-1, 2-2, and 2-3 — Sample Constructions

3. The Networking Letter   *26*
The Advantages of Networking — Letter Outline — Sample Letters

4. The Ad Response/Resumé Cover Letter   *48*
How to Create a Letter That Sets You Apart from Your Competition —
Letter Outline —
Killer Openings and Closings — How to Respond to Salary Queries —
Sample Letters

5. The Follow-Up Letter   *179*
How Follow-Up Letters Differ from Thank-You Letters — Letter Outline —
Killer Openings and Closings — Sample Letters

6. The Thank-You Letter   *201*
When to Send a Thank-You Letter — Letter Outline — Sample Letters

7. The Make Something Happen Letter   *214*
How to Jumpstart a Stalled Candidacy — Letter Outline — Sample Letters

8. Additional Jobhunting Letters 237

Reference Request Letters — Meeting Confirmation Letters —
Letters for Negotiating, Accepting, and Rejecting a Job Offer —
Letters of Resignation — Sample Letters

9. Killer Resources 250

Words and Phrases to Avoid and What to Use Instead —
The Cover Letter Checklist

Index of Letters That Address Specific Issues 254

Index of Letters by Industry and Job Title 255

Introduction

Of course, writing is tough. And writing about yourself is even tougher. Assessing your own strengths—honestly and accurately—is one of the most difficult tasks you'll ever face. When you're unhappy at work or out of work altogether, not feeling particularly good about yourself, it's even harder to do. Even if you muster up some terrific talents to talk about, like most people, you may be surprisingly shy about "tooting your own horn." You list your course work. You list your jobs. You list your job responsibilities. You list your hobbies. Finally, all you're sending prospective employers is a list!

But, employers don't want to hire a list; they want to hire a *person*. They want to hire a living, breathing human being. A personality. A humorous co-worker or a serious one. A team player or a self-starter. An intuitive thinker or someone who takes direction well. Sure, they want to hire a candidate with the appropriate skills, but they've got to like that person (YOU) too. After all, they'll be working together on a daily basis—and the better everyone gets along, the more productive the work will be.

What this means is that you must project your personality, or some aspect of it, from the very first ad you respond to and in the very first letter you write. The reason is that, to make a hiring decision, your next employer is looking for answers to three vital questions:

1. Do you have the skills this job requires?
2. Will you be compatible with my team?
3. Are you honest and willing to work, and do you have the right attitude?

Your resumé will answer the first question. Your letters, interviews, and references will answer the other two questions. Thus, your jobhunting letters are an essential opportunity to make yourself stand out as a unique and interesting person, someone an employer would like to meet, interview, hire, and work alongside.

To take advantage of this opportunity you must write well. And to get an edge over the competition you should not only write well, you should write often. Why? Most job applicants—your competition—never follow up after an interview. Of those who do, many write letters so inadequate that they actually impair what might have been a perfectly acceptable candidacy. Furthermore, most job search letters are forgotten after a quick review. What this means is that just writing your potential employer *at all* can put you ahead of other candidates. Writing a strong, impressive letter can put you miles ahead. And writing frequently can give you what advertisers call "top of mind awareness"; it can keep you on your next employer's mind no matter how long the hiring decision takes.

Unfortunately, for most jobhunters, facing that blank sheet of paper induces a terror matched by few other tasks. Be honest. Have you, at one time or another, ever found yourself following any of the Ten Most Common Steps to Writing?

Step 1. Panic: Your brain says, "I have to write."

Step 2. Procrastinate: You attempt your first escape by remembering that there is some equally pressing task that must be attended to, such as walking the dog, doing the dishes, calling Aunt Bella, or sorting the recyclables.

Step 3. Divert: You belittle the custom of writing such letters, wondering, "Why can't I just send my resumé?" Or "Why can't I just call and say thank you?"

Step 4: Delegate: You attempt your next escape by trying to get someone else to do it for you. "My sister's great at this; maybe she'll write it for me" is a common ploy.

Step 5: Panic again: You realize that you've got to get that resumé in the mail today and it's already 3:00 P.M.

Step 6, 7, 8. Shake, rattle, and roll: You stare at that cursed blank page, envision the finished product, and visualize all the heartache and strife you'll have to go through to get to that point. Then you picture yourself not getting the job because your letter sounded simple, unimpressive, unbusinesslike ("Whatever that is," you moan). So finally you go on a roll, recalling all the big business power jargon you've ever heard: "effectuate" ... "implement" ... "empowerment" ... "strategic envisioning" ... "global perspective."

Step 9. The mad dash: You furiously type these tired clichés on your last sheet of good paper, making your first draft your final one. As a result, in the end, all you can do is ...

Step 10. Mail, hope, and pray: And the greatest of these is pray.

Sound familiar? Don't despair, there is good news! Writing effectively is not as hard as you think. You don't have to be a Pulitzer Prize winning journalist. You don't have to use eight four-syllable words per paragraph. You don't have to make your correspondence any longer than it needs to be; writing voluminous letters won't guarantee you'll get hired. You have only to make yourself understood. You need to know what you want to say, and you need to say it clearly, accurately, concisely.

And that is precisely what this book will help you achieve.

This book is the product of our successful jobhunting seminar, *Jobhunter's Correspondence Workshop*, in which participants of all ages and professions secured a vital edge in their job searches. They discovered how to create more effective jobhunting letters and how to use letters more productively in their search for employment.

Many seminar participants wrote to let us know that they were using our techniques and achieving results. They were being selected more often for interviews and being offered desirable positions. Frequently we heard that a major benefit our seminar delivered was the simple encouragement to try something different in a letter. Openings that intrigue. Body copy that boasts. Formats that fascinate. We're delighted! We hope this book will do the same for you.

ACKNOWLEDGMENTS

We offer our heartfelt thanks to friends, colleagues, and family members who helped us in the preparation of this book. Your support enriched our undertaking by making our efforts seem significantly less taxing and infinitely more fun!

Sandra Podesta
Andrea Paxton

How to Use This Book and Disk

201 Killer Cover Letters is for any job seeker who finds it difficult to write the perfect cover letter—and that's almost all of us! This book tells you how to write every type of job search letter you'll ever need and puts at your fingertips a library of letters that will get noticed and get results. The special bonus disk contains all 201 killer cover letters featured in the book. You don't even have to rekey them—just change the specifics, and they're ready to send!

Before using the disk, peruse the book. If you're pressed for time, at least read Chaps. 1 and 2. Chapter 1 offers the basic do's and don'ts for writing effective job search letters. Chapter 2 helps you identify and position your strengths. Take a few minutes to complete Worksheets 2-1, 2-2, and 2-3 in this chapter. Doing so will furnish you with several powerful sentences you can use immediately in the body copy of your letters.

Then you can move on to the specific chapters that focus on the particular type of letter you're writing; in each chapter you'll find sample letters, as well as a choice of sample openings and closings. Each letter is titled with the industry or specific position of interest to the job seeker as well as issues addressed in the letter. For example, a heading such as WORKFORCE RETURN demonstrates that the letter is from someone returning to the job market after several years. SALARY indicates a salary discussion that may provide ideas for you to use. CONFIDENTIALITY refers to a request for discretion in contacting the jobhunter at his or her present place of employment ... and so on.

In addition to all the cover letters in the book, the disk also includes Worksheets 2-1, 2-2, and 2-3 from Chap. 2 for those who prefer to complete these on their computers. In using the model letters provided, it's important to personalize them so that they don't sound too generic.

Many of the company names and addresses, as well as the addressees' names, have been changed. The individual and company names and addresses in the sample letters are fictitious and any similarity to actual names and addresses is unintentional.

HOW TO COPY THE LETTERS AND WORKSHEETS
FROM THE DISK TO YOUR HARD DRIVE

Step 1: Insert the IBM-compatible disk into your floppy drive.

Step 2: Windows™ *Users:* From Windows Program Manager open **File Manager.** (File Manager is usually in the MAIN Program Group.) From the **File** menu, select **Copy** to open a Copy Dialogue box.

> **Helpful Hint:** In File Manager, make sure the **c:** folder is highlighted before copying the files. The c:\ folder is at the very top of the list of files in the c: drive.

At the **From** prompt, type: **a:**   (or the letter that refers to your floppy disk drive)

At the **To** prompt, type: **c:**   (your hard drive)

Press the **Enter** key, or click **OK**.

DOS Users: Go to the **DOS** prompt or the c:\ prompt.

At the prompt type: **xcopy a: c: /s**   ("a" is the letter that refers to your floppy disk drive; "c" is your hard drive)

Press the **Enter** key.

Macintosh™ *Users:* Use commercially available conversion software to convert the files on this IBM-compatible disk for your use.

HOW TO VIEW AND MODIFY WORKSHEETS AND LETTERS

> The directions provided below work with a variety of word processing programs. If you encounter any problems using this disk with your software, call the McGraw-Hill Technical Support Hotline at 1-800-217-0059.

Step 3: Open your word processing software, for example WordPerfect, Microsoft Word, etc.

Step 4: Use the book to choose the worksheet or letter on which you wish to work, identified by numbers (such as 4-9) at the top of the page on which it appears. The **c:\killer** directory you have copied to your hard drive identifies each worksheet and letter by the same numbers.

Your **c:\killer** directory houses subdirectories for each chapter in the book containing sample letters and one subdirectory for the three worksheets.

For example: **c:\killer\chap4\4-9**

c:	is your hard drive.
killer	is the directory in which the worksheets and letters are stored.
chap4	is the subdirectory housing all the letters contained in Chap. 4.
4-9	is the document name for Chap. 4's ninth letter.

Step 5: For some word processors: Go to the **File** menu and select **Open**. The Open Dialogue box will appear, giving you options for selecting directories, file names, and file types.

For WordPerfect: Use WordPerfect's File Manager (F5 for some versions of WordPerfect). Depending on the version of WordPerfect, you will either get a Dialogue box, a DIR prompt, or a Directory prompt.

Step 6: Select the **killer** directory on your hard drive and the subdirectory for the chapter in which the letter or worksheet is located (**chap4** in the example above).

For some word processors: Select your hard drive and the subdirectory in the Open Dialogue box.

For WordPerfect: Select your hard drive and the subdirectory in WordPerfect's File Manager. For some versions of WordPerfect, type **c:\killer** at the DIR or Directory prompt. This will bring you to a Dialogue box, which will allow you to select the subdirectory for the chapter. Highlight the subdirectory you want and press the **Enter** key.

Step 7: Select a worksheet or letter.

For some word processors: Type the document name (4-9 in the example above) at the **File Name** prompt.

If you prefer, in the Open Dialogue box you may use the **File Type** option to specify **All Files**. Or you can type *.* at the **File Name** prompt to display a list of all the letters in a specific chapter. Select the document name you want and click **OK**.

For WordPerfect: You will see a list of all the letters in a specific chapter. Highlight the letter or worksheet you want and press the **Enter** key.

Step 8: The letter you selected should now be visible on your computer screen. You can easily change, save, and print the letter using the appropriate commands for your word processor.

If you encounter any problems using this disk with your software, call the McGraw-Hill Technical Support Hotline at 1-800-217-0059.

Chapter 1

The Top Ten Rules for
Writing Killer Cover Letters

In the good old days, finding a job generally meant switching jobs. You sent out your resumé, went for an interview, and got the job. Why doesn't this work anymore? It's because these days, a resumé isn't enough.

In today's job market, a resumé doubles as a stop sign that signifies, "I need a job … like so many others … thousands of others." In this environment, your resumé alone cannot possibly accomplish as much as you need to accomplish. Although your resumé reveals vital statistics, it supplies only 20% of the information on which most hiring decisions are based. Your resumé reveals whether you meet the minimum requirements for the current opening (appropriate education, computer skills, or relevant experience, for example). Your resumé also suggests to your prospective boss the level of loyalty and continuity that can be expected of you as demonstrated by the length of time you've held previous positions. Finally, your prospective employer may attempt to reduce the list of candidates to a manageable level. In this case, your resumé may actually work *against* you by providing a single fact or date that serves to eliminate you as a potential employee.

Furthermore, regardless of how exceptional your resumé may be, it generally reveals none of the remaining 80% of information upon which the hiring decision is based. It says nothing of your personality, creativity, or work style. It rarely describes any unusual traits you possess that might make you a sterling candidate or interesting interview material. A letter, on the other hand, can reveal all of this—and more.

For all of these reasons, the letters you send as part of your job search may be some of the most important letters you'll ever write. To help you create a winning letter, let's begin with the basics. Take a look at a typical employment advertisement and the typical response it generates.

SAMPLE EMPLOYMENT AD

In today's economy, an ad like this one will receive between 300 and 1000 responses! From this pool, between 6 and 30 candidates will make it through the first screening to a personal meeting. Of these, between two and six people will be called for a second interview. Two or three will be selected as finalists. One will be hired.

Who will that be? Certainly *not* the person who sends in a resumé with Letter 1-1.

LETTER 1-1: RESUMÉ COVER LETTER SENT IN RESPONSE TO ADVERTISEMENT (POOR)

Dear Ms. Muldour:

In response to your ad in Sunday's paper, I have enclosed my resumé for your consideration. It is my objective to obtain a position in the economic area of your company. I recently received my MBA after completing a BS in Economics with a Business minor. I have an extensive background and strong working experience.

I would be very interested in working for your company due to the fact that it would permit me to utilize my business and economic background. In my six years of study, I have developed my knowledge of econometric analysis, price analysis, financial management, strategic marketing and business management. I am currently developing a paper on the treatment of trade tariff across county lines which uses a dynamic process and a flexible functional form to determine the variables affecting treatments among states. Working in a financial firm for several years enabled me to become a more committed leader, a team player, a detail-oriented worker, and better communicator who is not afraid to devise and implement effective strategic management theories. My responsibilities included researching the backgrounds of individuals and companies wishing to open sizeable credit accounts overseas. In addition, I have much additional working experience including a management trainer and busboy at a major dining establishment in New York City. I am a hard worker and a team player as you will see when you interview me. My resumé highlights my educational and business background.

As delineated on my resumé, I am fully functional in utilizing a complete range of microcomputing and main-frame operations including DOS, CPM, Lotus, Dbase III, DW370, Cobalt 500, Multimate, HG graphics, EconoMix, and FinFax programs.

Enclosed is a copy of my resumé for your consideration. Please don't hesitate to contact me at anytime for an interview. I am certain that you'll find it of great interest to meet me due to my natural leadership qualities, vision, and solid experience in your area of business.

Sincerely,

Philip Tucker

Philip Tucker

Because the majority of the people responding to this ad will not include a letter at all, simply sending this letter gives Mr. Tucker an advantage over the competition. The advantage is all but wasted, however, by sending a letter as weak and unappealing as this one.

As you read Letter 1-2, the following stronger version of the same letter, you'll see the differences—and the difference they make in the effectiveness of the letter.

LETTER 1-2: RESUMÉ COVER LETTER SENT IN RESPONSE TO ADVERTISEMENT (BETTER)

Terry Muldour
Box 34
Daily Gazette
City, State Zip

RE: Your ad in the *Daily Gazette* Sunday, March 3, 199X for a self-starter to help with financial planning

Dear Terry Muldour:

You're looking for a self-starter to work in the financial field -- I'm a self-starter with financial expertise and experience!

My resumé, which is enclosed, details my background; let me provide you with the highlights:

Thorough educational background: I recently received my MBA after completing a BS in Economics with a Business minor.

Firm grasp of finance: In my six years of study, I developed expertise in econometric and price analysis as well as marketing, financial and business management.

A proven self-starter: I am currently writing a post-graduate paper on various trade tariffs in the regional Northeast, for which I created my own unique research methods and models.

Financial work experience: By investigating individuals and companies wishing to open sizeable credit accounts overseas for Prudential Bache, I became a dedicated leader, a detail-oriented worker, and better communicator.

I am a hard worker and a team player. I have the knowledge, skill, and desire to enhance the success of today's financial company. If you will contact me at (555) 456-7890 during the day or evening, I will make myself available at your convenience for an interview.

Thank you for your consideration. I look forward to meeting you.

Sincerely,

Philip Tucker

Philip Tucker
(555) 456-7890

If you've hired someone yourself, you may recognize the weaknesses of the first, poorly presented letter—and the strengths of the second, stronger one. If you haven't hired anyone, approach the letter as you might a solicitation for a charitable contribution, a letter that attempts to be equally convincing. Which of the two letters would you be more likely to read through to the end? Which makes a better impression? Which candidate would you be more likely to interview?

TEN BASIC DO'S AND DON'TS FOR WRITING KILLER COVER LETTERS

The two preceding letters provide concrete, visual examples of the ten basic do's and don'ts to follow in all your jobhunting correspondence.

1. DRESS (YOUR LETTERS) FOR SUCCESS
Do send professional letters. Don't send form letters.

Do make your letters clean and professional looking. Even so much as an ink blot is clearly an insult to the reader. It implies that the reader is not worth the time it would take to retype the letter. Worse, it suggests that you are a sloppy person who doesn't value order, personally or in the workplace. Recruiters spend a good deal of time advising jobhunters how to dress for an interview because employers demand clean, orderly staff members with a professional demeanor. Your letter should reflect these characteristics.

Do not allow any letter to appear as if it were a form letter. The handwritten salutation at the start of Letter 1-1 suggests that the writer prints many copies of this letter and simply adds the recipient's name before mailing it. Your reader should not feel as though you are sending the same letter to hundreds of employers—even if you are! Instead, create the impression that you are sending a letter to a specific person for a specific reason: because you believe that there is an ideal match between you and your prospective employer. Standard lines such as "I want to work for your company" are meaningless to an employer, particularly if you haven't mentioned the name of the company as the writer in Letter 1-1 neglected to do. If you really want to work for a specific firm, you must have a reason. State it.

2. ZOOM, DON'T RESUME
Do make your letter different from your resumé.

If your resumé is strong, it will provide all the information your interviewer will need. (If it's not, there are plenty of books, software programs, and professional resumé writers to help you strengthen it.) So don't regurgitate your resumé in letter form. "Zoom in" on the most salient points of your resumé. Even better, consolidate facts in your resumé into an overview statement. Summarize a benefit—such as "solid employment record," "extensive industry experience," or "proven track record." Guide your reader in forming an appropriate impression of you even before you meet. Letter 1-2 illustrates this principle. Best of all, turn this sum-

4

mary statement into one that suggests an advantage your next employer may gain by hiring *you* instead of someone else.

Describe any special qualities that may set you apart from other candidates. Use language that creates a feeling of what kind of person you are. If you have a sense of humor, don't be afraid to show it in a professional way. You'll find examples in the sample letters throughout this book.

3. IN RESPONSE TO YOUR AD … *NOT!*
Don't use standard openings.

Many people think that only one type of letter is acceptable in the business world: one that follows a standard outline. In truth, the only type of letter acceptable in the business world is an effective one. An effective letter accomplishes your objective, which in the case of jobhunting letters, is to stand out from your competition. With this goal in mind, why send a letter likely to mirror the letters of those against whom you're competing?

Letter 1-1 opens with a standard line: "In response to your ad in Sunday's paper, I enclose my resumé for your consideration." What's wrong with this opening? It's standard, or in general use. To stand out from the competition, your letter should be anything but standard. In Letter 1-2, Mr. Tucker grabs the reader's attention immediately with a different opening. Furthermore, he successfully weaves information from the advertisement into the opening to suggest that the letter was written in response to a specific ad and is not a form letter.

Do not open your letter with a standard, predictable statement. Spend a few minutes analyzing what is important to the person to whom you're writing. Peruse the sample openings provided throughout this book. There's no need to be foolish, outlandish, or shocking. With thought and practice, you can create unique, informative letter openings that will grab attention and deliver a meaningful message.

4. "KISS" YOUR LETTERS (KEEP IT SIMPLY STATED)
Do write a person, not a letter.

There are also many people who believe that making a letter sound businesslike means using stuffy, stilted language full of clichés and jargon. Certainly, your letter should be professional. However, it must also be interesting, appealing, and reflect your personality.

To create a letter appropriate to the business world include relevant facts and succinct language. Ensure correct spelling and proper presentation. To make your letter appealing, use the same tone of voice you would use during the interview—when you don't have time to consult a thesaurus and replace the words you'd normally use with multisyllabic synonyms. Write with the attitude that you're writing to a person. That person may be your interviewer, your next boss, a human resources executive, or a recruiter—*but a person.* Before you write, try to picture him or her. Try saying out loud the points you wish to make as if you were sitting face to face in an interview, and then jot them down. Flesh out these ideas into full sentences that reflect the way you speak. After all, your interviewer will want to meet the person to whom she was introduced in your letter, and it had better be you!

For a clear example look back to Letters 1-1 and 1-2 by Philip Tucker. Letter 1-1 is replete with foggy jargon, leaving you without a single clear opinion of the candidate—except that he is likely to be boring. Letter 1-2 has introduced you to a person who has studied and is currently authoring a research paper, an individual with personality traits that sound appealing—someone you might not mind interviewing, which is, after all, the purpose of the letter.

You'll find words and phrases to avoid listed in Chap. 9.

5. ELIM-ME-NATE
Do focus on the needs of your prospective employer.

What do you talk about in your resumé? Me. Me. Me. Me. What do you talk about in your interview? Me. Me. Me. Me.

So use your letter to address the needs of your next employer. Focus your thoughts on the needs of your next boss. After all, your prospective employer expects you to meet *her* needs on a daily basis. Why should she care what your employment objective is or what you're looking for in a job? She will hire you and pay you for the specific contribution you will make to increasing profits, improving performance, or enhancing productivity. In the letter, tell her how you'll accomplish this.

Successful jobhunters create letters that link their strengths and talents to the benefits they bring to the firm, department, team, or supervisor with whom they'll be working. Chapter 2 is devoted entirely to illustrating how to achieve this crucial goal.

6. APPEALING IS REVEALING
Do make your letter easy to read.

The visual appearance of a letter is as vital as its content, maybe more so. Because if you're lucky, your reader will devote 30 seconds to your letter before turning to the next one in the pile. Make it easy to skim. Note that Letter 1-1 is boring in appearance. Its italic print and fully justified margins make it difficult to read. On the other hand, Letter 1-2 is visually appealing. Its content actually appears to be interesting and the letter can be scanned by the eye in seconds. The reader who spends 30 seconds on Letter 1-2 will form an instant, positive impression of the candidate.

How do you make a letter appeal to its recipient before he or she even reads it? Simple. You can use the same tricks that advertisers use. Sample Letter 1-4 on page 8 puts to use many of the proven formatting techniques upon which direct mail experts depend. But first, examine another unappealing, unrevealing letter on the following page.

Chief Financial Officer
P.O. Box 425
New York Times
New York, NY 10000

Dear Chief Financial Officer:

To maintain continued growth, a company must have financial and management professionals who are capable of identifying and seizing market opportunities before the competition does.

My marketing savvy and management expertise can help you do just that. I possess a powerful commitment to task, a drive for excellence, and the ability to respond to customer needs. For example, in my current position I increased sales 74% by upgrading service efficiency resulting in a 25% annual increase in profitability. I streamlined a branch outlet from ground zero, coordinating every aspect from recruitment to organizing and redefining office functions, thus achieving substantial cost reductions, greater efficiency, and increased market share. I reduced receivables from 115 days to 33 days, thereby improving cash flow 21%. This released enough working capital to enable the firm to expand into other markets. These achievements are certain to prove both valuable in and transferable to a range of firms.

Because I am currently seeking to broaden my horizons, I eagerly await your reply so that we can arrange a personal meeting. Then, we can discuss in greater detail how my particular blend of capabilities, experience, and managerial strengths can help your firm capture lucrative business opportunities.

Sincerely,

But take this letter word for word, format it differently, and the results are astounding.

Chief Financial Officer
P.O. Box 425
New York Times
New York, NY 10000

Dear Chief Financial Officer:

To maintain continued growth, a company must have financial and management professionals who are capable of identifying and seizing market opportunities before the competition does.

<u>My marketing savvy and management expertise can help you do just that.</u> I possess a powerful commitment to task, a drive for excellence, and the ability to respond to customer needs. For example, in my current position:

- I <u>increased</u> sales 74% by upgrading service efficiency resulting in a 25% annual increase in profitability.

- I <u>streamlined</u> a branch outlet from ground zero, coordinating every aspect from recruitment to organizing and redefining office functions, thus achieving substantial cost reductions, greater efficiency, and increased market share.

- I <u>reduced</u> receivables from 115 days to 33 days, thereby <u>improving</u> cash flow 21%. This released enough working capital to enable the firm to expand into other markets.

These achievements are certain to prove both valuable in and transferable to a range of firms.

Because I am currently seeking to broaden my horizons, I eagerly await your reply so that we can arrange a personal meeting. Then, we can discuss in greater detail how my particular blend of capabilities, experience, and managerial strengths can help your firm capture lucrative business opportunities.

Sincerely,

The difference between Letters 1-3 and 1-4 is not in the wording. The content of both letters is identical. The difference is in the formatting. Letter 1-4 employs many of the same techniques advertisers use to get millions of consumers to notice, absorb, and act on promotional messages. You can use the same tricks in your letters, which are equally promotional. Here are just a few of the more powerful options available to you.

- Adjust your margins so that the reader never has to read more than 5 inches from left to right across a page.
- Never justify your right margin. (Always justify your left.)
- Don't use long paragraphs; they are overwhelming to the eye. (This will help you write more succinctly, too.)
- Indent sections with key ideas by using bullets, dashes, or asterisks to set them off (like these indented tips).
- For important ideas use **bold,** <u>underlining</u>, and UPPERCASE LETTERS.
    - For short sentences, try centering.
- Use numerals (20) rather than spelling out numbers (twenty) when describing your accomplishments to attract more attention. (Exception: Always spell out numbers that begin a sentence.)
- *Italics are hard to read; use them sparingly, if at all.*
- If your letter must run to two pages in length, end the first page in the middle of a sentence to encourage the reader to read on to page 2.

If these techniques seem too pushy to you, remember that advertisers have been using them for decades *because they work!*

7. THE POSTMAN ALWAYS RINGS TWICE ... AND THREE, FOUR, OR MORE TIMES
Do write frequently.

Your competition hates to write as much as you do. Chances are that most of the people vying for your next job will find numerous excuses to avoid writing job-hunting letters. Don't make the same mistake. You should write these letters often. Always write a thank you letter for a referral, and a follow-up letter after a meeting or interview. If your candidacy seems to have stalled, write again to make something happen—don't allow yourself to be forgotten. You might send your prospective employer an additional reference, or a recent newspaper article supporting an issue discussed during your interview. As far as you should be concerned, until you get a definite rejection, you're still in the running. In many cases, this perseverance and follow-through are essential requirements for the job you want.

8. TELL THE TRUTH OR PAY THE CONSEQUENCES
Don't be dishonest.

Do not exaggerate, mislead, or lie in your letters. Even if you get hired, dishonesty is grounds for immediate dismissal. Don't risk it.

9. CHECK, RECHECK, AND TRIPLE-CHECK
Do triple-check your letters for proper presentation.

If you're new to the jobhunting process, you will find the following reminders helpful.

Do take the time to ensure that you've correctly identified the name of the company or organization. While we may refer to *Time* magazine, for example, as *Time,* it is actually one of the publications of Time Warner Inc. The manufacturer of the famous Reebok footwear is actually Reebok International LTD. What we call Prudential is correctly titled The Prudential Insurance Company of America. Disney is really The Walt Disney Company. Virtually every company in the United States is listed in *Standard and Poor's Register of Corporations,* which is published yearly. Most public libraries have such directories in their reference sections that list company names in full, and more for those who wish to do additional research. *Hoover's Handbook of American Business,* for example, provides overviews of most American companies, the products and services they offer, primary competitors and recent sales figures, the names and titles of key executives, addresses, and telephone and fax numbers for the firm's main headquarters.

Do direct your letter to the reader. Remember Terry Muldour from the sample employment ad earlier in this chapter? It was impossible to discern from the ad whether Terry Muldour was male or female. In fact, some recruiters purposely make an ad vague to test the resourcefulness of the jobhunter, a ploy Terry Muldour may have used. If you are faced with this ambiguity, don't rely on the standard "To Whom It May Concern" salutation because it's standard. Try to contact the company in question to obtain the information you need. If that fails, use the entire name (as did the writer of Letter 1-2) or the person's title (as did the writer of Letter 1-4).

Do check your spelling before mailing your letter. Poor spelling creates a sloppy, negative impression quickly. Proofreading backwards from the end of the letter to the beginning will help you catch errors that you might overlook when reading forwards. If you don't trust your own spelling abilities, ask a friend to proofread your letter. At the very least, use your computer's spell check program.

Do be sure to use the same paper type and color for your resumé, letter, and envelope. Your resumé and letters should bear the same heading—one that includes your name, address, and the telephone numbers at which you can be reached. (For printing purposes, the sample letters contained in this book do not have such headings on them—but yours should.)

Do check to be certain that you have matched the letter you send Ms. Smith with the envelope addressed to the same Ms. Smith. Always type names, titles, and addresses on each envelope; never hand address them. It's astonishing how many times jobhunters make these silly, but critical errors!

Do sign your letter. Recruiters report receiving a surprising number of unsigned letters. They do not report interviewing these forgetful people.

As bizarre as these examples may seem, they happen, and they can happen to you. To be sure they don't, triple-check your actions when it comes to jobhunting. The job search is not the time for accidental mishaps that can jeopardize your success. Chapter 9 contains a checklist to help you avoid such mishaps and to ensure that your letter is strong, direct, and properly presented.

10. IF IT AIN'T WORKING … FIX IT!
Don't keep using a letter that's not working.

You've composed a resumé cover letter, sent it in response to 10 newspaper advertisements, and haven't heard a thing; not a single person has called; not one interview has been scheduled. Is it you? Is it your resumé? It could be either. Or it could be that you're perfectly qualified, but your cover letter isn't making the impact you want. Worse, it might be hurting you.

Don't despair. Writing about yourself is never easy, and (until you've read this book) you've never been taught how to write self-promotional letters. Jobhunting letters may be some of the most difficult letters you'll ever create.

So if the letter you're using isn't working, try another approach. You can try a more unusual opening by adopting a bolder tone of voice or a more conservative one. You can also summarize your strengths more succinctly, or provide a bit more detail. The key is to try something *different*. Rewrite portions of your letter, and then send this new letter in response to new ads. If you don't get the results you want, try changing something else. It may take a while, but don't allow yourself to get discouraged.

By doing such things, you're employing the same tested marketing techniques that advertisers have used for ages. How many approaches and slogans has Burger King used? Or Ford? Or AT&T? These companies and their advertising agencies continually alter their strategic positioning to keep their profits up, their objectives met, and their goals achieved. Why shouldn't you?

Chapter 2

How to Identify and
Sell Your Strengths

Whatever industry you represent, field you're in, or expertise you possess, when you're looking for a job you're in sales and marketing. You're selling a product: you. You identify the target market: potential employers. You price the product: a realistic salary range. You position the product: draft a resumé and cover letter. You test your positioning with the target market: answering several ads. If your efforts result in interviews, you've probably done some decent marketing. If not, you'll need to reassess your product, market, pricing, or positioning, and try again. This is precisely the process that marketing executives follow to sell laundry detergent, pickup trucks, gourmet cat food, club memberships, and retractable swimming pool covers.

Thus, the majority of the letters you'll write in the course of finding your next job will contain self-promotion. In your Ad Response and Resumé Cover Letters you will trumpet your talents. After an interview, a Follow-Up Letter will once again reaffirm your excellent qualifications. If the hiring process seems to be idling, you'll rev that engine with a reminder of your unique talents. And undoubtedly, if you attempt to negotiate salary in writing, your special skills will be of vital importance.

Since self-promotion is an area in which recruiters have found most people either underwhelming or overwhelming, it pays to learn how to boast. It *is* possible to be modest, yet effective. The trick is to avoid speaking solely of your own merits in every line. Instead, link your talents to the concerns of the recruiter, employer, or firm. Think of your qualifications not as merely a feature of your candidacy, but as a *benefit* to your next boss. The worksheets that follow will help you accomplish this.

Take the time to complete Worksheets 2-1 and 2-2 right now. The ideas you jot down here will prove extremely useful when creating your own letters later on—whether you follow the guidelines offered in the chapters to come, or simply adapt the sample letters contained throughout the book. Completing these worksheets will also help you crystallize your thoughts in preparation for an interview.

WORKSHEET 2-1.: I AM ... BECAUSE I

In the left-hand column of the worksheet, list your skills, strengths, unusual abilities, unique traits, areas of expertise or specialization, and relevant personality traits. Try and limit your entries to one or two words each.

In the right-hand column, jot down your support points. Rather than repeating the facts on your resume, expand on them while relating something new, different, or additional. Consolidate your facts by adding together years in the field, jobs within an industry, or similar positions you've held at different firms. Summarize your career, education, experience, or personality. Follow the examples set by the three sample entries.

Go directly to Worksheet 2-1 on the next page. Or, complete this and the following two Worksheets on your personal computer by using the disk enclosed with this book. You'll find instructions for using the disk on pages x-xii.

I AM: (your skill, unusual ability, unique trait or area of expertise)	**BECAUSE I:** (how you acquired this particular strength)
I am *a skilled worker*	because I *worked at your leading competitor for over 15 years.*
I am *knowledgeable in word processing*	because I *studied at the Computer Training Center.*
I am *experienced in heavy equipment sales*	because I *was the Number Two biller for John Deere for three years and a top biller for General Motors for ten.*
I am	because I
I am	because I
I am	because I
I am	because I
I am	because I

With that done, you're now ready to seize a powerful advantage over your competition.

In their letters, those against whom you're competing are certain to include the type of facts you've written in Worksheet 2-1—facts like "I am a skilled worker," and "I am trained in using a word processor." Although these facts may be true, standing alone they require recruiters and employers to do all the work, that is, to interpret what these statements will mean to the company, to discern why they are beneficial.

You, however, can easily handle this for your reader. Simply ask yourself, "What does this mean to my potential employer?" Instead of just stating that you are a skilled worker, translate this fact into a benefit, such as "so you won't have to train me." To the statement "I am trained to use a word processor" you might add "so you save training time and money because I can begin being productive for you from day one." If you have chosen to cite the fact that you rarely take sick days, translate this into "Because I rarely take sick days, you can count on adding a very reliable worker to your support staff."

Therefore, to complete Worksheet 2-2, think about the benefits you can offer your next employer based on the statements you made in Worksheet 2-1. For each "I am" and "because I" you wrote on the preceding page, add a corresponding "And what this means for you is" in Worksheet 2-2 on the following page. As a guide, relate benefits to the areas that are of greatest concern to employers: profits, productivity, and performance.

Go directly to Worksheet 2-2 on the next page. Or, complete this and the other two Worksheets contained in this chapter on your personal computer by using the disk enclosed with this book. You'll find instructions for using the disk on pages x-xii.

... <u>AND WHAT THIS MEANS FOR YOU IS</u>:

(what benefits your skills, special traits, or background offer your next employer,
what positive difference or improvements you can make)

... so you *will save time and money since you won't have to train me.*

_____

_____

... so you *will have a worker who is productive from day one.*

_____

_____

... so you *get a sales representative who can hit the ground running.*

_____

_____

_____

... so you _____

_____

_____

... so you _____

_____

_____

... so you _____

_____

_____

... so you _____

_____

_____

... so you _____

_____

_____

Once you've completed Worksheets 2-1 and 2-2, you've identified your strengths and the facts that support them. More importantly, you've linked them directly to benefits you can offer your next employer. Now, you have successfully created unique ideas that you can introduce in your jobhunting letters. The sample letters in this book will provide many examples of how to do this.

Or, try to combine your entries from Worksheets 2-1 and 2-2 into full sentences. Use the sentences word for word, or reconstruct the sentence into alternative forms. The options on Worksheet 2-3 demonstrate how many ways there are to build a sentence describing the benefits you offer an employer.

Go directly to Worksheet 2-3 on the next page. Or, complete this and the other two worksheets contained in this chapter on your personal computer by using the disk enclosed with this book. You'll find instructions for using the disk on pages x-xii.

HOW TO USE THIS IN YOUR LETTER:
<u>**Benefit Statement Options**</u>

I am _____ because I _____.

What this means for you is _____.

Because I _____, I am _____.

What this means for you is _____.

Because I _____, I am _____

so you _____.

You (so you) _____ because I _____

_____ and I am _____.

You (so you) _____ thanks to my

(I am) _____ which I developed/became/achieved through/as

(because I) _____.

Through (because I) _____,

I have developed/built/become (I am) _____

and that means you _____.

Throughout my (because I) _____

I achieved/succeeded in/produced/excelled at (I am) _____.

As a result, you/The result is that you (so you) _____.

SAMPLE BENEFIT STATEMENTS

The following sentences have been composed from the three sample entries in Worksheets 2-1 and 2-2. Each sample uses one of the constructions outlined in Worksheet 2-3. For easy reference, these samples use the options in the same order in which they appear in Worksheet 2-3.

- I am a skilled worker because I worked at your leading competitor for over 15 years. What this means for you is that you will save time and money since you won't have to train me.
- Because I worked at your leading competitor for over 15 years, I am a skilled worker. What this means for you is that you will save time and money since you won't have to train me.
- Because I worked at your leading competitor for over 15 years, I am a skilled worker so you can save time and money since you won't have to train me.
- You will have a worker who is productive from day one because I studied at the Computer Training Center, and I am knowledgeable in word processing.
- You get a worker who is productive from day one, thanks to my knowledge of word processing, which I developed through my study at the Computer Training Center.
- Because I was the Number Two biller for John Deere for 3 years and a top biller for General Motors for 10 years, I have become experienced in heavy equipment sales and that means you get a sales representative who can hit the ground running.
- Because I am experienced in heavy equipment sales, I achieved superior results at John Deere and General Motors. As a result, you get a sales representative who can hit the ground running.

SAMPLE BENEFIT STATEMENTS ADAPTED FOR DIFFERENT INDUSTRIES

The preceding samples illustrate how three different people might build a variety of sentences from their completed Worksheets 2-1 and 2-2. Now take a look at how these same sentence construction options might be adapted for use in other industries. Although your field may not be one of those represented here, perusing these examples will demonstrate how you may adapt your own.

Engineer: I am a skilled electronics engineer because I worked in General Electric's Consumer Division for 4 years. What this means for you is that you will save time and money since you won't have to train me.

Arts: Because I worked at the Smithsonian Institute for more than 12 years, I am a highly experienced curator. What this means for you is that you will not need to be understaffed for weeks while training a novice to assume full curatorial responsibilities.

Sales: Because I worked at your leading competitor for over 5 years, I am experienced in all aspects of selling telecommunications to growing businesses so you can expect more immediate revenue growth from your sales team.

Sales: You get a sales representative who can hit the ground running, thanks to my experience in retail promotion, which I developed as a top account executive for Procter and Gamble.

Beautician: You will have a worker who is productive from day one because I studied at the Avalon Beauty Academy, and I am knowledgeable in all aspects of hair styling and coloring.

Sports: Because I was the senior ski instructor at Aspen Ski Resort for 7 years, I have become proficient in dealing with the public, and that means you get a representative who can significantly enhance customer relations.

Technician: Because I am well versed in maintaining 4- and 6-color printing presses, I achieved superior ratings at Dybold Paper Company. As a result, you acquire a technician who can minimize unproductive downtime for your company.

Use Worksheets 2-1, 2-2, and 2-3 and the preceding examples to create your own self-promotional sentences. Write one for each quality you will be promoting in your job search. Then, link these sentences together.

Voila! You have just written a paragraph (or two) that will constitute the body of many jobhunting letters.

SAMPLE LETTERS

By completing the worksheets, you have taken an essential step towards writing killer cover letters. As you incorporate the paragraphs you have just written into your letters, you are fulfilling Rule 2 from Chap. 1's "Top Ten Rules for Writing Killer Cover Letters": "Zoom, Don't Resume." This rule requires that you focus on the needs of your employer rather than simply repeating the information listed in your resumé. This advice holds true regardless of your industry, and the following sample letters illustrate this key point.

Take a few minutes to read these sample letters. You'll discover that they are very similar to each other. Each has been written in response to an employment advertisement in a different industry. Each is from an applicant in a different situation. They are presented here to illustrate that such details become immaterial when a letter "sells" a candidate, and how his or her skills might benefit a potential employer. Cover letters like these grab *and keep* a reader's attention. They stand a far better chance of resulting in an interview than the traditional, standard cover letters most people send.

Most of the sample letters included throughout this book illustrate this key principal. As you review them, you may be surprised at how little industry-specific, even job-specific information is included. So be sure you don't overlook letters that fall outside your field—virtually every letter in this book contains an idea you can use.

Ms. Presently Hiring
The Successful Bank
P.O. Box 1111
Business City, ST 09876

RE: January 1 <u>City Times</u> Ad
for a Bank Customer Service
Representative

Dear Ms. Hiring:

It's twice as hard to attract a new customer as it is to maintain an existing one. Unfortunately, this fact is often overlooked by many businesses.

> **Delivering high-quality, responsive service is vital in banking and that's exactly what you'll get when you hire me.**

As my resumé indicates, I have worked in financial services for more than 3 years so you won't have to go to great expense training me.

Plus, I have learned how to deal with a wide variety of people from the pleasant senior citizen to the irate executive. In every case, I assess their needs and how the bank can address them most effectively. The vast majority of my customers have walked away content. More importantly, they have <u>returned to do business with us again</u>.

If you're looking for an experienced professional to provide superior service and promote customer satisfaction, you've found her.

I hope you'll give me call at (555) 456-7890 so that we can meet. Thank you for this opportunity to discuss my qualifications.

Sincerely,

Ms. Presently Hiring
The Successful Company   RE: January 1 <u>City Times</u> Ad
P.O. Box 1111   for a Telephone Repair
Business City, ST 09876   Technician

Dear Ms. Hiring:

When a customer calls for a repair, your firm is faced with an opportunity. Either the client relationship will be cemented or it will be damaged. The difference, as you know, is in the hands of the repair technician.

> **The ability to deliver high-quality, pleasant service is vital in telecommunications and that's exactly what you'll get when you hire me.**

As my resumé indicates, I have worked as a technician for more than 3 years so you won't have to go to great expense training me.

Plus, I have learned how to deal with a wide variety of people from the pleasant senior citizen to the irate executive. In every case, I assess the complaint, the equipment problem and how I can address both most effectively. The vast majority of customers I have served have been pleased with my responsiveness and professional demeanor. More importantly, they have <u>continued to do business with my employer</u>.

If you're looking for an experienced professional to provide superior service and promote customer satisfaction, you've found him.

I hope you'll give me call at (555) 456-7890 so that we can meet. Thank you for this opportunity to discuss my qualifications.

Sincerely,

Ms. Presently Hiring
The Successful Travel Agency RE: January 1 <u>City Times</u> Ad
P.O. Box 1111   for a Travel Agent
Business City, ST 09876

Dear Ms. Hiring:

I am responding to your ad because it offers the opportunity to act on a very firm conviction: that every business is a service business and, to succeed, must address the distinct needs of each and every customer.

> **The ability to deliver high-quality, responsive service is vital in the travel industry and that's exactly what you'll get when you hire me.**

My resumé, which is enclosed, details my background. Although I have been out of the workforce for several years, I have hardly been idle. As a hospital volunteer, President of the PTA, wife and partner of a Senior Vice President, and mother, I have dealt with a wide variety of people from the pleasant senior citizen to the screaming child to the irate executive. In every case, I assess the individual's needs and how to address them most effectively.

As a very active consumer, I am well aware of the importance of prompt, attentive service -- and painfully aware that it is rare these days. If you're looking for a hard worker and quick learner to provide superior service and promote customer satisfaction, you've found her.

I hope you'll give me call at (555) 456-7890 so that we can meet. Thank you for this opportunity to discuss my qualifications.

Sincerely,

Ms. Presently Hiring
The Successful Hospital
P.O. Box 1111
Business City, ST 09876

RE: January 1 <u>City Times</u> Ad
  for a Mammography
  X-Ray Technician

Dear Ms. Hiring:

Delivering high-quality, responsive service is vital in health care and that's exactly what you'll get when you hire me. As my resumé indicates, I am licensed in this state and board certified. I have worked in clinics and in private practice for over 7 years, so you won't have to train me.

Plus, I have learned how to deal with a wide variety of patients from the pleasant senior citizen to the nervous mother and terrified single woman. In every case, I have provided comfort and reassurance along with clear instructions and a gentle touch.

> **In fact, the vast majority of patients with whom I work have walked away pleased with their care. More importantly, they have returned for their annuals year after year.**

If you're looking for an experienced professional to provide superior and proper care while dealing effectively with a diverse patient base, you've found her.

I hope you'll give me call at (555) 456-7890 so that we can meet. Thank you for this opportunity to discuss my qualifications.

Sincerely,

Chapter 3

The Networking Letter

The Networking Letter is also called the Prospecting Letter, the Broadcast Letter, or the Letter of Introduction. By whatever name you call it, it's indispensable.

Although few jobhunters choose to employ this valuable tool, networking should be the first step in your search—and your letters are integral to the process. Skillfully written and sent to the right people, Networking Letters can produce valuable information and promising leads. These letters can help you to identify job openings before they are advertised as well as the person with the authority to make the ultimate hiring decision.

To appreciate the edge the Networking Letter affords you, consider the marketing principle of action versus reaction. This principle, translated to the search process, characterizes people who *react* as those who wait for job openings to be announced and advertised; then they apply and wait again to be called in for an interview. The vast majority of jobhunters comprise this group and they are your competition.

Conversely, those who *act* create their own opportunities. They hunt down potential and existing job openings, and go after them with vigor, often identifying such openings well before they are advertised. Becoming one who *acts* rather than *reacts* places you in an important minority: that of confident proactive networkers. This is exactly where you want to be to enjoy a vital advantage in today's tough job market. As a proactive networker, you have priceless tools at your disposal in the Networking Letter. Use these tools wisely and frequently. To introduce yourself; to ask for advice, contacts, a referral to an associate or colleague. To identify openings before they are advertised, such as when colleagues switch jobs or companies or move to a new location and businesses ex-

---

| RECRUITER'S TIP |

HOW THE WORK WAS WON

Pull out the big guns and saddle up! In today's job market there are more job opportunities than job openings.

Fact: Only 25 percent of those landing full-time jobs learned of the openings through employment ads. The remaining 75 percent secured employment through active networking.

Networking is work ... but it's work that works.

pand. Even a company that is downsizing may hold promise by consolidating positions. Two specialized workers, for instance, may be replaced with one who can handle multiple responsibilities. You can use these letters to uncover this strategic information and more.

If a friend suggests you write an acquaintance for assistance, accept. If a newspaper or magazine article tips you off that a certain company might be hiring, ask if this is the case, and ask to be considered. Above all, don't be afraid to take advantage of these opportunities. Well written, such a letter presents you as a motivated, aggressive player who searches for ways to make things happen. In most every case, these qualities are highly sought after in the job market.

Whatever your reason for writing it, your Networking Letter is fundamentally an appeal for help. Your *Primary Goal*, your *only* goal, is to get your reader to comply with a reasonable request for assistance. You might ask for an introduction, a recommendation, advice, or ideas. To comply, your readers must give of their time, share knowledge, put their names or reputations on the line by making a referral—all precious commodities. To achieve your goal, you've got to convince your reader that you're worth this effort.

Follow the steps below to create effective Networking Letters. If you choose to use sections of the letters provided in this book, you can use these steps to adapt the samples for your own use.

STEP 1: CREATE A CONNECTION

To enhance the speed and effectiveness of your networking, you should send the Networking Letter to numerous people simultaneously. The trick, of course, is to make each letter sound as though it is being sent *only* to the person receiving it—your letters should never look or sound like form letters.

In your effort to personalize each letter, capitalize on any connection you may have with the reader. You may share an area of expertise. You may belong to a common professional association or civic, sports, religious, or charitable organization. You may have originated from the same area of the country or have attended the same educational institution. Now is the time to reaffirm these connections. Mention a mutual friend or a recent telephone conversation you had with your reader. If you met at a party or business event, remind her of the encounter.

Use this information to open your letter. Identifying a meaningful link between yourself and your reader helps establish a personal connection. Because this suggests to the reader that only he or she can help you, your reader will feel more compelled to focus on and reply to your request.

STEP 2: INFORM

To accomplish your primary goal, which is to elicit help, you must convince your reader that what you offer is meaningful. If you're asking for a referral, you must be worth referring. If you're asking whether there might be an opening for someone with your skills, your skills must be relevant to the firm, the division, or to the person you're writing. Keep in mind that recommending an unqualified candidate reflects poorly on the person referring you. Don't put anyone in this awkward position.

Therefore, in the body of your letter provide the information your reader needs to make the decision to act on your behalf. Describe your talents, your background, your skills. Explain why they are meaningful to your prospective employer, whether it's the person you're writing to or the person to whom you'd like to be introduced. And remember not to repeat word for word what's on your resumé, particularly if you'll be enclosing it with your letter.

How much space should you devote to this information? When asked how long a man's legs should be Abraham Lincoln observed, "Long enough to reach the ground." The same applies here: supply as much data as it takes to make your point convincingly, and no more. If the person you write is not the one making the hiring decision, keep your letters short and to the point. To secure a referral, for example, your reader needs to be assured in a general sense that you will not turn out to be unqualified, and, therefore, an embarrassment to him. Paint an overview of yourself that demonstrates that you have the necessary experience to be a serious candidate. When describing your background, generalize. When discussing your accomplishments, summarize.

However, if you're introducing yourself to someone who *does* possess the direct authority to hire you, you may wish to offer more detail. In this case, be specific about what you can bring to the corporation, the team, or your supervisor. Where relevant, use facts and figures to make your case—ones you can honestly support in an interview. Instead of listing your skills in a vacuum, link them to concrete benefits they offer your next employer. You may wish to refer back to the worksheets in Chap. 2 for pointers on how to do this.

In the samples that follow, you'll see examples of Networking Letters both brief and lengthy. As you read them, try and discern the reason the writer may have had for contacting each recipient. Apply this to your own circumstances, and you'll create a more effective letter.

STEP 3: REQUEST ACTION

You've established a personal connection. You've convinced the reader that you rate the time and energy required to comply with your request. Now, forge a bargain with the reader: "I'll do the work, if you're ready with what I need."

If you haven't already asked for whatever it is you want, now is the time to do so. State straight out exactly what you need, and how the reader can help you. Don't annoy your reader by beating around the bush. You should be polite, but also be direct. Your reader should not have to spend time deciphering puzzling innuendoes. If you're writing to introduce yourself, say so. If you're writing to ask for a referral, say so. Above all, don't ask for something that's inappropriate.

Then, **tell the reader what to do,** and be specific. If you've asked her to contact you, provide your reader with your address and telephone numbers for both work and home along with a time that is best to reach you. If you have a pager, cellular phone, beeper or answering service, supply instructions for using it. If you require confidentiality, say so. Make it as easy as possible for your reader to reach you. If you're asking that something be sent to you, include a fax number or a stamped, self-addressed return envelope.

Or, if *you* are the one who will take action, **tell the reader what to expect.** State exactly what you will do to facilitate a response. If you plan to contact your reader, say when, how, and why. If you're visiting from out of town, and would like to meet with your reader, state when you'll be in town and when you'll be available. If possible, offer several alternate dates and times.

OPTIONAL STEP 4: CLOSE WARMLY

It's highly advisable to end your Networking Letters with a professional, yet friendly sign-off. Closing warmly—by thanking the reader in advance for complying with your request—frequently enhances the likelihood of getting the response you seek. You'll find examples of such closings in the sample letters that follow.

Mr. William Danford
Assistant Vice President
Eastman Kodak
400 Eastman Way
Rochester, NY 09876

Dear Bill:

Can I ask a favor of an old fraternity brother?

The writer establishes the connection …

You see, in one way or another, this volatile economy affects us all -- and now it's my turn. Yes, I'm one of the 2400 loyal employees Camji has just laid off. So now I'm exploring options in our industry, including the possibility of launching a business of my own.

Your advice and perspective, Bill, would be very helpful to me as I decide what my next step will be. I'd appreciate it if you could spare some time to share your thoughts with me.

informs …

On the 25th of this month, I'll be in your area and would love to buy you lunch. I'll call next week to see if this is convenient.

tells the reader what to expect …

Thanks in advance -- hope to see you.

All best,

and closes warmly.

Bert

Ms. Annabelle Tisi
President
Economic Forecasting Association
350 North Wacker
Chicago, IL 09876

Dear Ms. Tisi:

As a 10 year member of the EFA, I am writing with the hope that our organization might assist me in my job search.

I am an experienced agricultural economist, with a specialty in soy and soy byproducts, seeking employment in either the private or public sector. I realize, of course, that I am not alone in my quest. However, as a prolific author, I can offer my employer a very high level of positive visibility within the industry.

Ms. Tisi, I would appreciate any advice you can offer. Does EFA, for example, maintain a job bank? Do you run a referral service? Perhaps you or an associate know of someone with whom I might speak for additional advice.

I would welcome any suggestions you can offer. Along with my resumé and a list of my published works, I've enclosed a stamped, self-addressed envelope in case there are any EFA materials you can send to me. To make matters even easier for you, I will plan to call you next week.

> *Make it easy for the reader to comply.*

For your interest and assistance, I am deeply grateful.

Your fellow member,

Anthony Amend
(555) 765-4321 work
(555) 456-7890 home

Ms. Nancy McCauley
Arlington Data Products
36 Kennedy Street
Arlington, Virginia 09876

Dear Ms. McCauley:

A mutual acquaintance, Shirley Louis, recommended that I contact you for advice. I am currently exploring the possibility of entering the data processing field after 12 years in medical equipment sales. With your expertise in data processing and your recent experience entering this field, you have insight that could prove extremely valuable to me.

I've enclosed my resumé, which details my skills and background, along with a list of my accomplishments. I expect that several of my strengths will be quite transferable, such as attention to detail and the ability to work with complex technology. I would welcome your views on this observation, as well.

Knowing how busy you are, I would be most grateful if you could spare a few moments of your day for me. I will call your office shortly to arrange a meeting at a time that is convenient for you.

With appreciation,

Ethan Nichols
(555) 456-7890 extension 45

Although the writer is not required to provide this information, she feels the reference to daycare will alleviate any concerns her reader may have about reliability.

Ms. Angela Reese
Staffing Director
Massachusetts Municipal Hospital
1840 Wilmont Avenue
Shireville, MA 09876

Dear Ms. Reese:

I am writing at the suggestion of Francis Myers, a maternity nurse on your staff and a close friend of mine. Francis thought that your needs and my talents would fit ideally, and that we should meet.

By way of introduction, let me explain that I am returning to nursing after a three-year absence. During this time, I had a son and relocated to the Boston area. Now that I have made arrangements for day care, I am seeking to put my skills back to work where they are needed: in a Burn Unit. My **solid training** and **in-depth experience** have both focused on the care of burn victims and I would like to return to my nursing specialty as soon as possible.

I will take the liberty of calling you next week to see if we might meet. If you would be kind enough to leave word with your assistant, I will schedule a meeting at your convenience. In the meantime, I thank you in advance for your consideration.

Sincerely,

Elizabeth Morris
(555) 765-4321

Mr. William M. Mackey
Assistant Treasurer
CitiTrust Bank
505 Pratt Street
Wilmington, Delaware 09876

Dear Bill:

What a small world! Ten years ago, you and I worked at United Savings and now our paths have crossed again. It was great seeing you at the Clearinghouse luncheon last week; I appreciate your offer to pass my name along to your EFT people.

To this end, I've enclosed my resumé which details the considerable experience I've enjoyed in funds transfer, including my key role in the development of EFT systems for two major commercial banks.

As you no doubt recognize, this kind of hands-on expertise can prove immensely valuable for you and for CitiTrust. It means that I am equipped not only to forecast the challenges that lie ahead as our industry continues to evolve, but also to create the <u>innovative solutions</u> demanded of those banks that will succeed in the years to come.

I am making plans to visit Wilmington from the 5th through the 15th of next month and would love to get together with you. I will call your office shortly to set up a meeting.

Thanks again, Bill, for your interest.

Sincerely,

Carolyn Marie

Ms. Delilah Vimond
Director
The Artists Alliance
15 Center Park Drive
Oakhurst, IL 09876

Dear Ms. Vimond:

Because you graciously added your name to State University's Alumni Career Network, I am writing with the hope that you might spare a few minutes to advise a fellow alumnus.

I earned my BS in Accounting at State, and have since enjoyed a successful career in the sales and marketing of consumer electronics and telecommunications. Now, I would like to bring the benefits this solid background offers to a new field. Your role in the arts community, Ms. Vimond, could provide a perspective on this transition that would be of great value to me.

Because I would appreciate the opportunity to gain some of your insight, I will take the liberty of calling you next week to see if we might meet or simply speak on the phone. In the meantime, I have enclosed my resumé to provide details.

I am grateful for your willingness to help fellow State graduates. I thank you in advance for helping me, in particular.

Most sincerely,

Bill Johnson
(555) 765-4321

This is actually a combination Networking/Make Something Happen Letter; notice the writer's clever suggestion to overcome the interviewer's hiring objection.

Ms. Constance O'Neill
The New Orleans Symphony Orchestra
80 Newtown Square
New Orleans, LA 09876

Dear Ms. O'Neill:

Meeting you was a real pleasure. Thank you for spending so much time with me, particularly on a Friday evening. I truly appreciate the advice you gave me and the contacts you offered.

Since our meeting, I have reworked my resumé according to your recommendations; a copy is enclosed with this letter. I am thrilled with the new emphasis and have forwarded it to Maestro Richard Allen at City Orchestra, as you suggested. I will let you know the results of these efforts.

Ms. O'Neill, I am dismayed that you are not currently able to hire an Assistant. Not only would it be a pleasure to work with you, but I am certain that my corporate background could open new doors for The New Orleans Symphony Orchestra. Should my experience produce the level of additional funding I anticipate, the position of Assistant would certainly pay for itself!

Ever the optimist, I will keep in touch with you in the event the Orchestra's financial status improves.

Thank you again for your kind assistance.

With best regards,

Anna Rodriguez
Work Phone
Home Phone

Mr. Colin Curtis
Executive Vice President
NationsTrust Bancorporation
Chicago, IL 09876

Dear Mr. Curtis:

When last we met, we spent some time discussing the inviolability of the Glass-Steagal Act. Lo and behold, just three short months later, our legislators are considering overturning this venerable standard!

Therefore, I thought you'd be interested in seeing the enclosed article, featured in the *Economist*'s current issue, which analyzes the effect such a dramatic move would have on banks' consumer investment base. Obviously, now is the time to devise proactive strategies to keep this profitable market from eroding, and the article highlights the actions several financial institutions have already taken.

Mr. Curtis, I thought of you immediately upon reading this article because I found our discussion so enlightening. I also appreciate the interest you expressed at that time in my attempts to further my career. I am continuing my search and will keep you informed. In the meantime, should your firm's hiring freeze be lifted, I hope you will think of me. Your organization has been at the top of my wish list for years, and, after meeting you, I am certain that our association would be immensely productive for us both.

Thank you again for your interest.

All best,

Pauline Sinclair
(555) 765-4321

Enclosure

Mr. James J. Milstein
Assistant Treasurer
Chase Manhattan Bank
14 Chase Plaza
New York, NY 09876

Dear Mr. Milstein:

It was a pleasure meeting you at last week's Retirement Seminar. The amount of work that went into preparing such an informative program was evident and well spent, I can assure you. Your presenters held the interest of each participant, and clearly described the products and services your firm offers.

Given my background and interest in this dynamic area of financial services, I believe that I may be able to offer your firm something of value in return. As the enclosed resumé demonstrates, my track record with prospective customers is a proven one; over the last 16 months, <u>I have increased our company's sales of retirement planning services by 22%</u>!

Mr. Milstein, this is the growth potential I would like to offer a leading firm such as yours. If there is any advice or recommendation you could offer, I would be most grateful. I will take the liberty of calling you shortly to see to whom I should address my credentials at Chase.

Again, my thanks for a most enjoyable seminar and for any assistance you can provide.

With appreciation,

Peter Anselmo
(555) 456-7890

This letter may produce freelance work, a referral, or an interview. Any of these could lead ultimately to a job. That's effective networking.

Mr. Martin Dupree
Southwestern Technologies
6700 Industry Circle
Dallas, TX 09876

Dear Mr. Dupree:

It was with great alarm that I read in today's *Wall Street Journal* that you are forced to curtail your in-house promotional capabilities. Undoubtedly, today's economy wreaks havoc without regard for individuals, families, or profits. Despite this unfortunate situation, may I offer a glimmer of hope?

> With reduced staff and financial resources, it becomes ever more essential to generate **free publicity,** and to do so requires an expert.

I can deliver this critical service without an office at your headquarters, without an administrative assistant on your payroll, without costly health care benefits. For a modest per-project fee, I am available to identify newsworthy developments, to draft press releases and place them with appropriate media representatives for **maximum, free exposure.**

Mr. Dupree, in today's rollercoaster economy, the need for publicity is more vital than ever. Don't let your firm drop from sight -- or worse, receive only the negative attention that results from a story such as today's *Journal* piece. I will call shortly to follow up.

Sincerely,

Lydia Bruner
(555) 456-7890

Note the Killer Close!

This writer obviously knows her reader well so a familiar tone of voice is an appropriate choice.

Ms. Erica Martin
Schaeffer Industries
1442 Lansing Street
Detroit, Michigan 09876

Dear Erica:

It is hard to believe how long it has been since we have been able to sit down and talk. How about scheduling lunch (on me) before another day passes? Here's my ulterior motive right up front: I have a thought on which I'd love to get your advice.

Since we started working together over a decade ago things have changed dramatically. Technology, people, places and things seem to be in a constant state of flux. (I suppose this is what makes life interesting.) Through this flux, my firm has remained alive and well, continuing to break new ground in the world of electronic design. Nevertheless, I have been giving some thought to relinquishing the freedom of self-employment for the security of a staff position.

Perhaps, in your travels through the winding roads of corporate America, you may have heard what firms are hiring? If any? Are companies likely to outsource design projects or acquire staff with an eye towards cutting costs? These are the questions I'll need to answer before making my decision. I know your viewpoint will be beneficial.

A nice, soft approach

I'll call you early next week to set up a lunch date. Can't wait to see you.

Best,

Beth Wadell

Ms. R. Susan Shapiro
The J.J. Budd Catalog Company
800 Budd Promenade
Stonington, CT 09876

Dear Ms. Shapiro:

You may recall that last May I had the pleasure of working with you when you were at AmeriBrands for several weeks. I was delighted to hear from our mutual friend, Mark Miller, that you might be looking to hire a telemarketing sales supervisor.

No one can dispute J.J. Budd's supremacy in its field. I believe, as I am sure you do, that superior telemarketing is an integral part of J.J. Budd's continued success. After four very successful years at AmeriBrands I am now looking for new challenges in the telemarketing industry. I would like a chance to be part of your telemarketing sales team -- and to achieve for J.J. Budd the impressive results I have attained for AmeriBrands:

> **As my resumé indicates, during my 4 years as a Sales Manager with AmeriBrands, I consistently earned a place on the list of Top Ten Sales Managers. I also trained and ran the farm data TSR team that achieved the lowest cost per order among three competing vendors.**

For a number of months, I have worked with Mark Miller. Mark can vouch for my abilities to motivate TSRs and achieve high sales at a low cost. Please feel free to talk with him. (Mark's number at work is 800-555-7654 extension 123.)

I will give you a call in the next day or two to see if there is a convenient time we can meet to discuss how my accomplishments might benefit you and The J.J. Budd Catalog Company.

Very truly yours,

Raj Rammanvihal
(555) 765-4321

Ms. Nelda S. Wilcox
Anderson Industries
98-761 Tremaine Avenue
Portland, ME 09876

Dear Ms. Wilcox:

Thank you for your warm response to my cold call! It is gratifying to know that there are, indeed, executives who remember their own early career struggles.

As promised, I've enclosed my resumé and a list of my accomplishments. Any advice you can offer on the presentation of both would be most appreciated -- as is your kind offer to introduce me to your colleagues.

Together, my education and experience equip me to quickly grasp the intricacies of the business world. My talents allow me to apply this knowledge to the ways in which I can most directly contribute to your profitability and performance.

I will follow up shortly to discuss your reaction to the enclosed materials. Thank you again for your consideration.

Sincerely,

Brita Porthanoy
(555) 765-4321

This extremely enterprising student has set her sights on the firm she wishes to join after graduation and the executive she believes will usher her in the door. She's certainly not afraid of working hard to get what she wants, as this letter demonstrates.

Ms. Judith L. Seifert
Redfield Industries
43980 Corporate Park
Elizabeth, New Jersey 09876

Dear Ms. Seifert:

Redfield Industries' striking profit margins have captured the attention of everyone in the business world -- and I am no exception. Congratulations!

Although the story behind this tremendous growth has been told over and over by the media, no one has focused on your contributions, Ms. Seifert.

As staff writer for State University's respected daily newspaper, I would like to focus on your perspective as a female executive, and the unique way in which you have contributed to Redfield's success. Rest assured, I will not waste your time. Not only have I done my research on the company's track record, I am also a chemistry major with a special interest in the groundbreaking innovations Redfield Industries has introduced in air purification systems, in which you played a key role.

I would be honored if you could spare some time from your busy schedule to speak with me. I will call you shortly to see when we might meet.

Thank you in advance for your time.

Sincerely,

Marla S. Pirski
(555) 456-7890

Ms. Helen Muir
FronTech Systems, Inc.
605 Technology Drive
Columbus, OH 09876

Dear Helen:

When I heard through the grapevine that you had joined FronTech, I was thrilled for you! I know that you've been anxious to find the ideal position, and I truly hope that this is it.

Although FronTech has a sterling reputation, I know that you'll find some way to improve its standing. After what you achieved for MVRS, I can only say that the competition had better look out!

And, Helen, since I currently work for one of those very competitors, I thought this might be the perfect time for us to be on the same team. (After all, if I can't beat you I might as well join you.) If you are or will be in the position to add to your staff, I hope you'll keep me in mind. As you know, my track record is exceptional, my achievements legendary, and my motivation as strong as ever. (OK, so my modesty needs work.)

Before you get ensconced in management meetings, let me buy you lunch. We'll celebrate your new job and explore what the future may bring. My treat.

I'll call you next week.

Best,

Ruth Miller-Syms
(555) 456-7890

Mr. Alan Wang
Wang, Malone and Lee
2468 South Terrace
Grand Rapids, MI 09876

Dear Mr. Wang:

I am writing you at the suggestion of my father, Jon Omura, with whom you are a member of the Winchester Club. My father has spoken highly of your firm's summer internship program and, as a result, I would like to explore this unusual opportunity further.

For a Business major like myself, such a program would offer valuable hands-on experience in the real world. More importantly, the chance to learn from experts such as those you employ is the chance of a lifetime.

Mr. Wang, would it be possible for you or one of your colleagues to spare some time to speak with me about your unique summer program? I have attached my resumé to assure you of my strong qualifications.

I will take the liberty of contacting your assistant, Michael Fields, next Tuesday morning to see whether I might set up an appointment.

I thank you in advance and send my dad's greetings.

Sincerely,

Jason Omura
(555) 456-7890

Mr. Barry Fine
Director of Training
United Manufacturing Company
5200 Milton Park
Lincoln, NE 09876

Dear Barry:

What a thrill it was to participate in your Productivity Seminar last week. My congratulations on a highly informative and very entertaining presentation. I am quite certain that if my department placed as much emphasis on our clients' perceptions as you do on presentation materials, we would be far more productive!

Which is exactly what leads me to write to you. Observing you in action reminded me of my past life in training. Through repeated promotions, I have been elevated away from my real loves: instructing, encouraging, identifying, and then developing potential among bright, eager minds. I guess the more I crunch numbers, the more I lose sight of the people producing them, and it's been long enough.

Barry, before I leap, I should make sure there's water in the pool, so to speak. Here's the deal: I buy you lunch, you endow me with your view of the training game. I would really be grateful to hear your views. I'll give you a call next week to see whether you can make the time for me.

And thanks again for a stirring presentation.

Best,

Shirl Rebrussin

Mr. Perry Alban
Jones, Miller and Roberstson
5376 Valley Drive
San Bernadino, CA 09876

Dear Perry:

It's been a while since we've seen one another. I hope all is well with you, Linda, and your two spunky boys!

You may have heard that I recently married and now have a baby on the way -- and this is why I'm writing. Now that I am a family man myself, I am searching for a position in the restaurant/hospitality business that is more career-oriented, one that offers benefits and security.

As part of my search, I am writing to my colleagues and friends to see whether anyone might be aware of hiring activity, either current or planned. If so, I would be grateful if you could pass my name along -- or let me know who to contact.

Perry, after 20 years in the business together, you know my broad-based experience and the skills I offer. I am an industrious worker who takes interest in my work and pride in my performance.

Any assistance you can provide will be greatly appreciated.

All best,

Lincoln H. Nelar
(555) 456-7890 home

Resumé enclosed

Chapter 4

The Ad Response/ Resumé Cover Letter

Whether it's sent unsolicited or in response to an advertisement, through a referral or to a friend as part of your networking efforts, your Ad Response and Resumé Cover Letters afford you an important opportunity. With this letter you create the context for your resumé. A well written letter serves as a road map for the route a potential employer will take through the winding facts, figures, and dates on your resumé. In an effective Cover Letter, you can draw a conclusion for your reader that is supported by the data contained in your resumé.

In all cases, the *Primary Goal* you seek to achieve in your Cover Letter is to make your reader want to meet you and to interview you. Your letter should introduce you as *more* than simply the list of qualifications and accomplishments on your resumé. It should bring you to life as a three-dimensional person who is interesting and unique. It must make your reader want to meet the person presented in the letter … YOU!

RECRUITER'S TIP

START AT THE TOP

Serious jobhunters don't write only in response to ads in the "Help Wanted" section of Sunday's paper. They create their own opportunities.

If you have identified a firm that may be hiring someone with your skills, write directly to the Department Manager, Division Head, or Company President.

Letters get filtered down the corporate ladder—they rarely make their way up.

Your *Secondary Goal* is to predispose your reader to make a connection between your skills and his or her needs. If you are responding to an employment advertisement, you may have a good idea what qualities your prospective employer is after. If you have an understanding of the job requirements from past experience, you can use this perspective to highlight your own individual qualifications. The worksheets in Chap. 2 demonstrated how to link your specific talent with the needs of the hiring firm. In the sample letters that follow, you'll see how to incorporate this skill into your Ad Response and Resumé Cover Letters.

As you peruse the sample letters, you'll discover that virtually every one features an opening line you may think of as somewhat unorthodox. Think again.

STEP 1: GET ATTENTION

Your Ad Response or Resumé Cover Letter arrives on your prospective employer's desk in one of two ways. Either it arrives unsolicited, such as when you send your resumé after hearing about an opening or through a referral; or it arrives with hundreds of other resumés from your competition, as when you answer an employment advertisement.

Once it does arrive on that desk, it's fighting for attention against all those other resumés and letters, plus the usual reports, memos, and mail. The person to whom you are writing may give your correspondence a full half-minute, perhaps only 5 or 10 seconds, for a quick scan. As a result, you've got to win that reader's concentration immediately, like direct mail advertisers do when they print enticing messages called "legends" on a mailer's outer envelope and a headline at the top of the letter. You can do the same.

Forget the standard openings you used to use—you know the ones that are used by the vast majority of jobhunters such as, "In response to your ad in the *Daily Times*, I enclose my resumé for your consideration." While this opening may be appropriate for use with some highly formalized firms and industries or when writing to foreign organizations, a line like this is a wasted opportunity for most people jobhunting in a competitive economy.

Instead, begin your letter with a strong opening line that suggests to the reader, "Hey, read me!" Or, even better, "Don't hire anyone until we've met and I'll tell you why."

RECRUITER'S TIP

RE: THE RE:

Recruiters often place ads for more than one job opening at a time. Rather than sacrificing a strong opening line to refer to the ad you're answering and where it appeared, incorporate this information into your letter (see Letter 4-1). Or, simply add an RE: at the top of your letter like this and in Letters 4-2, 4-3, and 4-4:

RE: Your ad in the October 3
     <u>Daily Times</u> for an Office
     Manager

The first line of your letter should accomplish one of three objectives. The first is to **promise a benefit** to the reader. Tell your next employer what advantages you'll bring to him such as any unique skills you possess, a rare perspective you offer, or a proven track record. If your fluency in a second language is pertinent, mention it. If you are familiar with new systems or equipment, say so. Just be certain that what you offer is meaningful to the firm and to the position you seek— and that you can really deliver what you promise.

A second way to open your letter is to **identify a need** that your reader has. For example, your reader may be searching for someone who knows a specific production process or piece of equipment. Perhaps the need is for someone already familiar with the ins and outs of the business, the industry, the competition, or relevant government regulations. If you're writing to an accountant looking for an assistant, for example, you might open your letter with: "As an accountant, you know the importance of keeping abreast of changing government regulations. In my position with the state legislature of New Jersey, I managed such information on a daily basis."

A third objective for your opening is to **be timely.** Use your opening to relate news or new information. Refer to a recent event or issue of concern. Tie the end of the old year or the beginning of the new to the opportunity you offer for a fresh approach. Where appropriate, mention a new law, trend, report, newspaper article, or the current economic climate.

KILLER OPENINGS

The following sample openings illustrate how each of the three objectives discussed above is achieved.

Promise a Benefit:

- In the last 12 months, I've generated $40,000 worth of new business for my employer, and now I'd like to do the same for you.
- As a computer expert skilled in combining numerical data with appealing graphics, I can provide the support your staff needs to bring in new business while saving you money on outside consultants.
- Integrity. Motivation. People Power. That's what it takes to be a successful manager. And that's what you get when you hire me.
- Your ad for a translator caught my attention immediately. *Pourquoi? Perche? Porque yo soy la persona perfecta por la position.*
- They say there's no rest for the weary. So if you're weary from overwork, forget the rest of the candidates. Hire a proven professional, like me, who can relieve you of your overwhelming workload and help you get the rest you deserve.

Identify a Need:

- For the opening in your production department, why not consider an expert who has spent the last three years mastering state of the art film equipment at MTV?
- You're seeking a hard worker ... I am. You need retail experience ... I've been in the business for 15 years! You ask for references ... I've got plenty.
- If you're looking for a top-notch dental assistant, look no further.
- The match between your needs and my talents is ideal. Why? Because ...

50

Be Timely:

- No one has money to burn in a tough economy—which is why adding one exceptional research pro to your staff can actually reduce your overhead. Allow me to explain.

- If the federal government approves the revision of PL-1442 next month, you'll require the skills of a collections agent who has dealt with hazardous waste—a rare expertise I'd be pleased to offer you.

- Congratulations on your recent promotion! With the additional responsibilities this entails, you may need an assistant with the special expertise I can offer you.

- In today's economy, there's no time to waste on workers who need continual training, motivation, and fires lit under them. Why not hire an experienced self starter like me?

STEP 2: INFORM

It's in the body of your letter that you support the promise you've made in your opening. Here is your chance to explain why the person or the company should consider, interview, and hire you. If you have completed the worksheets in Chap. 2, you already possess several strong concepts to use for this step in your Ad Response and Resumé Cover Letters. If you haven't completed these worksheets, take a few minutes to do so now, or follow the guidelines below.

First detail any specific skills, talents, or knowledge you possess and what difference this will make to the firm—without repeating point by point what's on your resumé. If your abilities might help your immediate superior reach his goals, say so. If you're switching fields, explain the benefits this offers your prospective employer such as a new perspective, or the opportunity to expand into new areas.

Then, describe how you will deliver the benefits you've promised, or how you acquired the special skills you possess. State what experience has taught you, and how you learned. If you accomplished relevant goals in previous jobs, use this to support your claim; where appropriate use dollar amounts, percentages of growth, or increase (and be sure you can substantiate them if you're asked during the interview). Relate work experience to skills acquired, and not to job responsibilities. Relate school experience to skills or knowledge acquired, and not to specific coursework. If you're switching fields, note similarities between your current or previous job and the job you seek.

STEP 3: INSTRUCT

You've grabbed the reader's attention. You've detailed your support points. Now for the next section of your letter. Here is where you tell your reader how to take advantage of the offer you've made, or the advantages you've promised. After all, if you're going to participate in the hiring process, you've got to tell your reader how to reach you.

Generally this can be handled quickly and simply. This is not to suggest, however, that this part of your letter is unimportant. On the contrary, *instructing* is all too often overlooked or rushed through by jobhunters ... and it's a shame. This step is as important as your opening. Why? Because the likelihood that your correspondence will achieve the response you desire increases with each additional word, and with each additional line your reader reads. So if your reader is still with you at this point in your letter, chances are she's interested in you. Therefore, you want to get her while her interest level is high. What's more, the simpler it is to take the next step, the greater the chance that step will be taken. Therefore, you want to make your instructions easy to understand, and even easier to follow.

To get the reader to respond to your letter you've got to **tell the reader what to do,** and be specific. Provide a complete address and telephone number at which you can be reached. State whether the phone number is a work or home number.

RECRUITER'S TIP

DON'T PLAY HARD TO GET!

A strong letter can make your reader want to contact you immediately. Don't miss this opportunity! Always position your telephone number so that the reader can't miss it. Place it:

- Prominently at the top of each page of your resumé.

- As part of your letterhead.

- In the body of your letter.

- Under your name and signature.

If you prefer to be called during certain hours, say so. If confidentiality is an issue, ask your reader to maintain it when contacting you.

If the next step is going to be *yours,* you've got to **tell the reader what to expect.** Be equally specific about what you will do. Say when you'll follow up. Say how you'll follow up: by phone, by mail, by express mail, by messenger. Tell the reader what information you're enclosing with your letter, if any. If you'll be forwarding additional material, say when you will do so, or when it should arrive.

Finally, the hiring process will stop dead in its tracks if you don't follow up as you have promised. So do.

You'll find examples of this vital step in virtually every sample letter in this book. Here are just a few:

Samples of Instructing

- I look forward to hearing from you. My address and telephone numbers are listed above.
- I will wait to hear from you. My direct line at work is (555) 765-4321. Or you may call me at home at (555) 456-7890.
- I will await your response. You may reach me at home (555-456-7890) or at work (555-765-4321).
- I hope you will contact me in the very near future. I am anxious to discuss the possibility of working together. You'll find my address and telephone numbers listed below.
- Because my current employer is unaware of my job search, I would appreciate it if you could contact me at home during the evenings at (555) 456-7890.
- Please feel free to call me evenings at my home or to leave a message on my answering machine. My home number is (555) 456-7890. (My present employer is unaware of my job search.)
- I'll contact your office shortly to see when we might meet.
- I'll call your assistant on Wednesday of next week to set up a meeting.
- I'll be in town throughout the month of December, and will contact you to schedule an appointment.
- I'll give you a call on the 18th of this month to set up a meeting. In the meantime, please feel free to contact me at (555) 765-4321.
- I will send my references to your office by messenger first thing tomorrow morning. If there is anything else you need, please let me know. My work number is 555-765-4321.
- You should receive my resumé and recommendations by express mail tomorrow. I will call your office in the early afternoon to verify that they have been delivered.

OPTIONAL STEP 4: CLOSE WARMLY

The fourth and final section of your letter is the closing. Unless your correspondence is a short, hard hitting letter, you should generally add some final line before your "Sincerely." You might thank the reader for taking the time to read your letter or for considering you as a candidate.

The following sample closings will help you out in a variety of jobhunting situations, as will the many examples contained in the sample letters through this book.

Sample Closings

- I look forward to hearing from you.
- I look forward to meeting with you at your earliest convenience.

- I thank you for your consideration.
- Thank you for your interest.
- I would welcome the opportunity to work with you.
- I would welcome the opportunity to contribute my skills to your firm/team, and look forward to speaking with you soon.
- I'd like to put my expertise to work for you.
- I'd be pleased to demonstrate my abilities first hand.

HOW TO RESPOND TO SALARY QUERIES

Frequently, employment advertisements ask you to reveal your current salary, or your salary history. Should you do it? What you should *not* do is to ignore the question. Prospective employers may assume that your salary requirements are too high to be realistic, or too low to admit. They may assume you feel above answering their queries, or that you are less than thorough in your efforts. If they assume any one of these things, you're out of luck.

How should you handle this irksome issue? An excellent strategy is that used by the author of the letter on page 55, written in response to an ad in a trade publication, which read "Serious candidates will provide salary history."

This writer knew that the ad would generate a great deal of interest, and produce a multitude of responses. She also realized that the employers would be looking for ways to reduce the number of candidates to a reasonable size, such as rejecting those who ignored the request for a dollar figure; rejecting those whose salary history was too low to indicate a sufficient degree of authority in past jobs, or whose salary expectations were too high. She believed that stating a specific figure could eliminate her immediately from consideration. Furthermore, her primary goal in writing this Cover Letter was to secure an interview, during which she would have the opportunity to discuss benefits, perks, and other issues affecting salary. As you'll see in the final paragraph of her letter, she effectively shapes a deal with her reader: If you give me what I want (an interview), I'll give you what you want (a salary discussion). In this way, she has not avoided the question of salary. Instead, she used it to her advantage. In fact, she was selected to be interviewed.

There are other options, as well. You may simply state that salary is a negotiable issue for you, one that you will be happy to explore in an interview. If you feel compelled to include a dollar figure, you may prefer to give a broad salary range, or state an amount that reflects your total compensation (some combination of salary, bonus, anticipated raise, incentives, benefits and perks such as a car, expense accounts, club memberships). Your industry may dictate the way in which you will calculate such a figure. For instance, someone who works only three days each week might calculate what her salary would be if she worked five days. A teacher might calculate what his annual salary would be if he earned it for 12 months rather than the nine he actually teaches. Whatever you decide, be sure you can substantiate it during the interview.

Mr. James Milton, Vice President, Sales
Ms. Marie Bruno, Advertising Director
Fashion Clearinghouse
44 West 44 Street
New York, NY 10000

Dear Mr. Milton and Ms. Bruno:

I am applying for the position of Marketing Communications Supervisor because your ad said these three things to me:

- Your thoughtful, classy layout -- setting it apart from all the other ads on December's <u>FashionWeek</u> Help Wanted page -- "beat the clutter," the dream of all retailers.

- Your description of the ideal candidate reflects <u>my</u> skills, <u>my</u> strengths, <u>my</u> experience.

- You are a substantive company offering a product of superior quality.

My resumé, which is enclosed, speaks of my experience and expertise in retailing, and most recently in the marketing of personal computers. I am assertive, diligent, driven, and hardworking. I am a seeker of end results -- and I achieve them, as the enclosed overview of my accomplishments proves. I thrive <u>and deliver</u> in a demanding, and fast paced environment. I am willing to tackle and accomplish any project. My management style is open, humorous, example-driven, and loyal.

Sells personal strengths

I believe that we can be successful partners. I want the chance to meet with you and would consider an interview a most wonderful opportunity. I'll make myself available at your convenience so that we may discuss salary in detail, and I can provide references.

I look forward to hearing from you.

Sincerely,

Aldo Clement

SAMPLE LETTERS

The following pages contain samples of well written Ad Response and Resumé Cover Letters, many of which were written in response to employment advertisements. Peruse these samples to find ideas that appeal to you or inspire you as you create your own "killer" letters. As you do, keep in mind the following important points:

Summarize. Generalize. Customize. The letters included here represent a variety of industries and positions. Nevertheless, you'll discover that our writers have summarized, generalized, and customized so effectively that many letters would work equally well in other fields. Don't be surprised that you don't find endless details, facts, and dates—all that is resumé material! These letters focus less on listing specific experiences, and more on providing an overview of those experiences and an interpretation of the benefits such experiences offer a potential employer. Your letters should do the same.

Use the Disk to Copy ... It's Perfectly Legal! When you bought this book, you purchased the right to copy and adapt part or all of the letters in it. In fact, the PC disk that accompanies the book is designed to simplify this for you! By all means, use the samples provided here, although you may wish to adapt them in the event your interviewer or competition uses the same letter.

Name, Rank, and Serial Number. Due to space constraints, in many cases the samples provided do not show each writer's name, address, and phone number. Remember to include this vital information on every letter you send.

This and the next few letters are ideal for those who like to get right to the point.

Mr. Presently Hiring
Vice President
The Successful Company   RE: Your ad for a
P.O. Box 1111   _____(position)_____
Business City, ST 09876   <u>City Times</u>, 11/20/9X

Dear Mr. Hiring:

I urge you not to hire anyone until we've met. That's because I possess every one of the seven qualifications you list in your ad -- and more -- as the enclosed resumé reveals.

The sooner we meet, the sooner I can begin producing results for you, your team, and your company. Why not give me a call at (555) 456-7890 during the day or evening? I will be pleased to meet with you at your convenience.

Let's get together!

Sincerely,

Name

Mr. Presently Hiring
Vice President
The Successful Company   RE: Your ad for a
P.O. Box 1111   (position)
Business City, ST 09876   City Times, 11/20/9X

Dear Mr. Hiring:

The hiring process is tough enough without interviewing countless candidates who responded to your ad despite being underqualified or overqualified. I can save you from this onerous, time-consuming task.

As my resumé indicates, I possess every one of the qualifications you seek, and I am available to meet with you at once and begin working right away.

Why not give me a call and streamline what might otherwise be a lengthy interview process? I look forward to hearing from you.

Sincerely,

Name
Work Telephone
Home Telephone

Mr. Presently Hiring
Vice President
The Successful Company
P.O. Box 1111
Business City, ST 09876

RE: Your ad for a _____(position)_____, <u>City Times</u>, 11/20/9X

Dear Mr. Hiring:

With responsibilities and deadlines that won't wait, why spend valuable time interviewing unqualified candidates?

As you'll see on the enclosed resumé, I have the educational background, professional experience, and track record for which you are searching. In addition, I am motivated and enthusiastic, and would appreciate the opportunity to contribute to your firm's success.

I can promise that meeting with me will not be a waste of your time—and I will make myself available at your convenience, during or outside of normal business hours.

Sincerely,

Name
Work Telephone
Home Telephone

Mr. Presently Hiring
Vice President
The Successful Company
P.O. Box 1111
Business City, ST 09876

RE: YOUR AD FOR A _____ (POSITION) _____,
CITY TIMES, 11/20/9X

Dear Mr. Hiring:

An innovative company like yours thrives because it hires innovative thinkers like me!

Over the years, I have developed a reputation for introducing fresh approaches to solve the challenges faced in today's competitive business world. Because this is a personality trait -- not a learned skill -- it is one I can offer your firm with confidence. It is who I am. It has defined the contributions I have made in every position I have held.

My resumé, which is enclosed, begins to tell my story. A personal meeting with you will supply vivid details. The references I'll provide will support them.

Please call me at (555) 456-7890 to schedule an interview. I promise you won't be disappointed.

Sincerely,

Name

Ms. Presently Hiring
The Successful Company
P.O. Box 1111
Business City, ST 09876

RE: Your ad for a _____(position)_____, <u>City Times</u>, 11/20/9X

Dear Ms. Hiring:

The educational background, experience, and skills listed in your advertisement are only the beginning of what I can bring to your firm.

As you'll see on the outline of accomplishments I've included with this letter, I have a solid history of producing results within a limited budget. I have built and successfully managed a staff of 20, and I deal effectively with customers, executives, and stockholders on a regular basis. All of these achievements are critical to firms, such as yours, that must compete in today's difficult economy.

My resumé is enclosed as proof that I meet all the criteria listed in your ad. An interview would give me the chance to further prove my unique strengths.

I hope to hear from you shortly.

Sincerely,

Name
Work Telephone
Home Telephone

Ms. Presently Hiring
Vice President
The Successful Company
P.O. Box 1111
Business City, ST 09876

RE: Your ad for a _____(position)_____, <u>City Times</u>, 11/20/9X

Dear Ms. Hiring:

In today's challenging economic climate, many people will respond to your advertisement. Few will be interviewed. One will be hired.

However ...

Of the many to respond, few will be as qualified as I am, having 12 years of in-depth, bonafide industry experience. No one will bring my track record and the expertise I can offer—expertise that equips me to start delivering results for you <u>immediately</u>. With minimal training. With minimal disruption. With maximum positive effect for your bottom line.

I will make myself available to meet with you at your convenience. Thank you for your consideration.

Sincerely,

Name
Telephone

Enclosed: Resumé

This is a gutsy approach, balanced by the tactful reference to "unavoidable cost cutting" and supported by solid, relevant experience.

Ms. Melinda Ovett
President
Ovett Electronics
970 East Park Avenue
Merritt, WI 09876

Dear Ms. Ovett:

Because I have long admired your achievement in building a successful company, I was dismayed to learn of your recent layoffs. In today's economy, such a situation presents the vexing conundrum: how to maximize opportunities for growth with diminished human resources?

Opening identifies a need.

Optimizing the resources you <u>can</u> employ is, of course, a viable solution -- one I can offer if you would grant me the chance to meet with you.

When we meet, you'll find me to be a person with a positive outlook who enjoys identifiying ways to make something work rather than reasons not to try. This perspective is invaluable in setting an example for employees who are called upon to assume numerous responsibilities -- of particular merit in this era of unavoidable downsizing and cost cutting.

In addition, my resumé (which is enclosed) demonstrates that I possess the background and experience our industry demands, and your success deserves.

Ms. Ovett, if I have taken great liberty in writing to you, it is because I firmly believe that I can contribute to your firm's continued expansion. I will call you early next week to see whether we might get together.

Sincerely,

Stan Harding
(555) 765-4321

Director, Human Resources
P.O. Box 1111
City Times
Brigham City, AK 09876

To the Director of Human Resources:

Good opening when ad does not provide a name.

Four years in college and what have I learned? Plenty! Plenty that I can apply directly to the entry level position you advertised in this Sunday's City Times.

The drive to focus and achieve: Your firm's success depends upon the ability of your staff to grasp a problem, evaluate the best way to solve it, and then work until the solution is in hand. This is precisely the process I followed all four years to graduate with a 3.80 average.

Flexibility and creativity: A business gets stale when it continually recycles the same ideas time and time again. When you hire me, you get someone who thinks for himself, and who is not afraid to suggest new ways to approach a task as I did as the Student Representative responsible for researching and updating State University's Ethics Standards to reflect the difficult issues facing today's students and faculty.

The ability to work with a diverse population: Having been raised in an ethnic environment, educated in a multicultural institution, and with a degree in Psychology, I am well equipped to interact productively with customers and staff from a variety of backgrounds, with a range of priorities, and from the stockroom to senior management.

An interview would grant me the opportunity to demonstrate my abilities. I will call you soon to see if we might meet. Or you can reach me at the number listed below.

Thank you in advance for considering me.

Sincerely,

R. Alexander Conen
(555) 456-7890

Idiom International
P.O. Box 478
777 Central Avenue
Santa Rosa, CA 09876

Great line when responding to a P.O. box.

To the Placement Experts at Idiom International:

With my fluency in Mandarin Chinese, French, and English, I can help businesses operating in today's global marketplace acquire a broader customer base as they enhance their international identities.

With my in-depth experience in the travel and entertainment industry (as detailed on the enclosed resumé), I can offer these firms the opportunity to serve more customers, from more cultures, more personally, more appropriately than ever before.

With your strength in worldwide placement, you can help us both profit by successfully matching my rare qualifications with the needs of a growing firm.

I will call you Monday to see if we might schedule an appointment. I look forward to meeting you personally.

Until then,

Cheng Liu
(555) 765-4321

Ms. Judith Benjamin
President
Benjamin Personnel, Inc.
100 Fifth Avenue
New York, NY 10000

Dear Ms. Benjamin:

I appreciate your willingness to assist in my job search. As promised, I have enclosed my resumé to provide background on my professional experience. To bring my resumé to life for you, allow me to tell you more about myself and what sets me apart from other candidates.

Over the years, I have performed in a variety of environments. As a result, I have been exposed to diverse people, work styles, standards of measurement, corporate cultures, and demands. What has remained consistent throughout is my ability to produce results in a range of business climates.

Turns negative into a positive.

I have contributed to the success of management teams and worked on my own without supervision. I have mastered the ability to deal with frustrated customers, management under pressure and companies operating in the midst of labor negotiations and layoffs. Throughout, I have received consistently high praise from superiors and co-workers, many of whom are ready to serve as references, should you wish to contact them.

Enhances credibility.

To an employer, I present a positive, results-oriented work ethic and professional, pleasant demeanor. To you, I present a strong, solid candidate with a willingness to remain flexible in terms of salary requirements.

I will contact you next week to continue our discussion and to solicit any advice you may offer in my search. I thank you again for any help you can provide.

Sincerely,

Joanna DeMettriano
(555) 765-4321 day or evening

How to respond when an entry level position is barely described or the company unnamed? This letter and the ones that follow provide some answers.

Director, Human Resources
P.O. Box 1000
The City Times
Lincoln, NE 09876

To the Director of Human Resources:

Your ad for an Entry Level position caught my attention as I prepare to begin my professional career upon graduation this spring from State University.

I say "professional" because I have worked steadily throughout college, gaining valuable experience that equips me to present your firm with advantages others may not offer.

For example, as a Resident Assistant for a 250-person coed dormitory, I acquired strong leadership and interpersonal skills. I am now able to think quickly on my feet in emergency situations, and in those requiring quick assessment of many factors in order to make appropriate decisions. Dealing with the diverse concerns of students, parents and faculty, I have become adept at operating with the proper mix of authority, diplomacy, and tact.

Translates life experience to employers' needs

While working in this demanding position, I achieved a 3.75 cumulative grade point average. My double major, Communications and Political Science, provided me with a thorough foundation in principles that affect businesses every day.

I would welcome the chance to discuss openings at your firm. If you will contact me at (555) 456-7890, we can schedule a meeting.

Thank you for your consideration.

Sincerely,

Bert L. Vymer, Jr.
(555) 456-7890

Resumé enclosed

Director, Human Resources
P.O. Box 1000
City Times
Wynfair, PA 09876

To the Director of Human Resources:

Enclosed with this letter is my resumé, which details my education, work experience, and computer capabilities -- all important criteria in your search to fill the entry-level position that you advertised.

Allow me to introduce the person with whom you and your colleagues will work, should you choose to interview and hire me.

I possess strong moral and ethical principles, which led me to put in long, hard hours at school and part-time jobs in order to succeed in a challenging educational environment. These values also motivate me to perform diligently and loyally to contribute to my employer's profitability. Unlike others, I do not expect to begin as a Vice President. I know that it takes commitment, dedication, and intelligence to rise within a firm, all of which I offer you.

As one of six children, I also possess an active sense of humor, which has been useful in defusing difficult situations. I have the patience to see an assignment through to completion. I am comfortable delivering presentations to a group, working as part of a team and helping others succeed.

It would be an honor to meet with you personally to discover more about the opening at your firm and how I can assist your organization in its growth. Please contact me at the address or phone number listed above. I will make myself available at your convenience.

Thank you.

Sincerely,

Noreen Schimmer

Director, Human Resources
P.O. Box 1000
<u>City Times</u>
Boulder, CO 09876

To the Director of Human Resources:

For the entry-level opening at your firm, why not consider someone like me with a strong academic background and real world business experience? As you'll see on the enclosed resumé, I have recently completed my undergraduate studies at State University. My perseverance and consistent effort enabled me to maintain my Dean's List status while working on a part-time basis.

Rather than work at a mindless job that might pay the bills but teach me little of practical value, I chose to open and operate my own painting company. I selected and trained crew members, developed an advertising program, borrowed the money to cover start-up costs (which was repaid in full after just 6 months); and handled scheduling, payroll, and tax reporting. Over the five years I've been running my business, I have served more than 80 different customers, 54 of which have called us back to complete other jobs.

My experience has prepared me to meet the demands of the business world, and I am anxious to apply my strengths and talents in the corporate environment. I would appreciate the opportunity to meet with you to explore this possibility.

Thank you for considering me.

Sincerely,

Joseph E. Reed
(555) 765-4321

Resumé enclosed

Mr. Sanford J. Alexander
Vice President
P.O. Box 1000
<u>City Times</u>
Harrisburg, PA 09876

Dear Mr. Alexander:

The background and experience I can offer in reply to your ad for an entry level position in sales may prove ideal for your needs. Allow me to introduce myself and my qualifications.

This June, I will receive my Bachelors of Science degree in Psychology from State University. In addition to my rigorous course study, I participated in several extracurricular activities that provided me with the kind of hands-on experience that is so vital to a successful Sales Representative.

As Rush Chairman for my fraternity, I planned and directed a major program to introduce the strengths our product delivered, and promote them in a market ripe with competition. Through these efforts, we enjoyed an <u>increase in membership of 20% over the previous three years</u>. I further developed and managed a program to raise funds for our non-affiliated charity, the Brothers of Hope. Targeting fraternity members, students at large, faculty, and the community, the program <u>generated contributions that exceeded previous years' totals by 77%</u>.

To achieve these goals, I combined an ability to plan, to creatively visualize solutions, and to successfully implement them with my talent in dealing with people. These are the same characteristics I would bring to an organization such as yours.

Please consider me a serious candidate for your sales position. I will be happy to visit your offices for an interview. I can be reached at the telephone numbers printed below.

Sincerely,

L. Robert Cummings
School Telephone Number: (555) 765-4321
Post-Graduation Telephone Number: (555) 456-7890

Director, Human Resources
American Business Machines
46-890 St. Andrew Road   RE: Your Ad for an
Baltimore, MD 09876   Entry Level Position

To the Director of Human Resources:

When my mother and father sent me from our village in China to
America, I was fortunate to live with relatives who encouraged me to
excel -- and I have. I quickly mastered English, a new culture, acquired
exceptional computer skills in high school, achieved and maintained a
3.50 average at State University.

When I was granted a full scholarship, I was fortunate to have the time
to devote to volunteer work in addition to my studies. I served for four
years on the University's Community Relations Board as a liaison
between the school, neighboring politicians, residents, and businesses.
This valuable experience prepared me to deal effectively with
consumers, business clients, shareholders, co-workers, and executives at
every level of management.

When I graduate this May, I will be fortunate once again if I have
secured employment with a firm such as yours. My ability to work
productively with others, drive to excel, and unique cultural perspective
equip me to become a valuable member of your organization.

I hope you will contact me to arrange an interview so that I can provide
you with additional information to supplement what appears on my
resumé (enclosed).

I look forward to hearing from you.

Sincerely,

Dawn Cheung
(555) 123-4576

Ms. Nancy Lange
City Times
P.O. Box 1234
Lincoln, NE 09876

RE: Entry Level Position
City Times, Sunday July 5, 199X

Dear Ms. Lange:

This past May, I graduated from State University Magna Cum Laude with a 3.80 average, having financed 100% of my college education myself. As you can see, I am not afraid of hard work and would welcome the chance to discuss with you the entry level opening at your firm.

My resumé is enclosed to describe my academic background and professional experience. As you'll see, my 4 years of solid work experience exposed me to substantial interaction with consumers. I consider myself skilled in dealing with the public and would prove a positive representative for your firm.

In working summers on the Alumni newsletter, I learned to coordinate an inordinate number of facts, figures, dates, and details -- under deadline pressure!

These skills, combined with the drive to work through difficulty towards the successful completion of a project will make me a productive addition to many organizations. If you think yours is one to which I can contribute, please let me know. I'll come in at once for an interview.

Sincerely,

Marie Delusia
(555) 456-7890

Resumé enclosed

Mr. John Brunella
Vice President
First Federal Savings of Boston
7650 Revere Street
Boston, MA 09876

Dear Mr. Brunella:

Your associate, Amy Levin, advised me that she has sent you my resumé so that you may consider me as a 199X participant in First Federal's training program. I have enclosed another copy of my resumé for your convenience.

On May 25, I will graduate from State University with a major in Economics, a minor in Business Administration, and a concentration in Mathematics. I am planning a career in financial services, for which my education has ideally prepared me.

Ms. Levin and others have spoken highly of your firm's training program. It is precisely the type of challenge I seek. In return, I offer First Federal a loyal and hard working employee who already possesses a solid foundation of relevant knowledge. Unlike other applicants who may have a more general education, my training would allow me to be a highly productive member of your training program. As a banker, I would be able to more quickly put this supplemental training to profitable use for the Bank.

I would appreciate the opportunity to meet with you. I can be in Boston any Friday this semester, or any day after graduation.

I look forward to hearing from you and thank you for your consideration.

Sincerely,

Gloria Ashford-Washington
(555) 456-7890

cc: Amy Levin, Assistant Treasurer
    First Federal Savings of Boston

Vice President
Bernstein Enterprises
P.O. Box 1111
Newark, NJ 09876

RE: Your ad for a
Customer Representative
City Times, 1/20/9X

Appropriate salutation when ad bears no name.

To the Vice President:

As a State University senior who will be graduating in May of 199X, I am answering your ad because I believe I can offer your firm an unusual mix of abilities, talents, and enthusiasm.

For instance:

- My double major (Economics/English Literature) demonstrates my willingness to assume more than the typical level of responsibility and to achieve in a challenging environment.

- Through my coursework, I acquired in-depth computer proficiency and a profound belief in the importance of effective communication on today's growing entrepreneurial endeavor.

- To finance my education, I planned, launched, and operated a highly successful catering business. I gained hands-on experience in properly managing revenues, time, and employees.

As you can see, I am goal-oriented, driven, and not afraid of hard work -- qualifications vital to anyone who will be a productive staff member for your firm. As I would like to be.

I look forward to hearing from you so that we may schedule an interview.

Sincerely,

Bill T. Pasini
42 Chestnut Street
555-456-7890

The Groton Legal Forum
900 San Bernadino
Los Angeles, CA 09876

Dear Associate:

What a wonderful service you provide! Placing qualified professionals within the legal profession serves the needs of many, particularly someone like myself who is entering the field with so much to offer.

As I near completion of the ABA-approved Paralegal Program at State College, I am preparing to offer my skills to Los Angeles County law firms. In addition to my superior, straight-A record in this program, I possess a background in the business world that arms me with a valuable perspective others may not have.

For 20 years, I was an integral member of Digital Electronics' product innovation team. In this capacity, I worked closely with federal regulators and patent attorneys, and I can bring this experience to bear on behalf of your clients.

Also, I am trained in automated legal research programs (Lexis and Westlaw), and maintain my student password.

I would welcome the chance to pursue any openings for which you feel I may be qualified.

Sincerely,

Marion LaMarca
(555) 456-7890

P.O. Box 1000
<u>City Times</u>
New York, NY 09876

**RE: Entry-Level Paralegal Position
advertised in the <u>City Times</u>, June 6, 199X**

An entry-level position is not *de facto* fillable only by the inexperienced. On the contrary, in me you have a talented professional available for part-time or full-time work.

Having performed in a range of capacities in law firms both large and small, as the enclosed resumé reveals, I can offer you a wealth of legal capabilities, including:

- Contract preparation, negotiation, and administration in support of legal counsel.

- Ability to serve as an independent contract paralegal and investigator, as I have for many different attorneys and firms in the metropolitan area.

- Comprehensive paralegal skills, obtained through practical experience as well as in study leading to Paralegal Certification at State College.

- Experience with the use of an Office Automation System, WordPerfect, Microsoft Word, Lotus 1-2-3, and Prodigy.

I would appreciate the opportunity to interview with you and can make myself available at your convenience.

I thank you in advance for your consideration.

Sincerely,

Mark Jensen
(555) 456-7890 work
(555) 765-4321 home

Ms. Joanna Moore
Ralston, Mine & Lewis
123 Walnut Street
Atlanta, GA 09876

RE: 5-15-9X <u>City Times</u>
    ad for a Paralegal

Dear Ms. Moore:

This August I will be relocating to Atlanta where I hope to continue serving as a paralegal. My work with first-rate attorneys equips me to offer you an exceptional mix of training, knowledge, experience, and professionalism.

As you'll see on the enclosed resumé, I have worked for several law firms in the Philadelphia area. I am proficient in many areas of criminal and civil trials with an additional concentration in contracts and titles. As a result, I can offer you an unusual level of expertise in researching complaints and discovery requests as well as responses to counterclaims, motions for discovery sanctions, motions for summary judgments, and motions to dismiss.

The attorneys with whom I work have provided me with superior recommendations to aid me in my search. I would appreciate the opportunity to present these to you, and introduce myself as a candidate for the position at your firm.

Supports candidacy.

Ms. Moore, I will be in Atlanta at the end of this month. If you will contact me at (555) 765-4321 during the day or evening, we can schedule an appointment.

Thank you.

Sincerely,

Howard M. Melman
(555) 765-4321

Ms. Julia Robb-Joyce
Joyce Public Relations
98 Reading Avenue
Lenghorn, PA 09876

Dear Ms. Robb-Joyce:

Voila! You've found the Administrative Assistant you're looking for in me.

I have all the qualifications listed in your ad ... and more! My experience is relevant and extensive, as described on the enclosed resumé. My typing is exceptional and I can work in Powerpoint, WordPerfect for Windows, and Lotus.

What my resumé cannot illustrate is <u>what sets me apart from other candidates</u>. Namely, my penchant for organization, my eye for detail, my positive and personable nature, and my ability to perform -- even in the pressure cooker environment of a fast paced, fast growing international public relations firm.

Brings her to life!

Furthermore, I am fluent in French, with fair skill in German, having been raised in a multicultural family. These language abilities will help you in dealing with international customers and prospects, as will my familiarity with foreign customs and protocol.

I would be pleased to come in for a personal meeting. I will call you shortly to set up an appointment.

Merci,

Angelicque Lapin
(555) 456-7890 work
(555) 765-4321 home

While maintaining her professionalism, this candidate allows her sense of humor to shine through—a refreshing change from the many other letters the ad produced.

Ms. Adrienne R. Hilman
Rivers, O'Sean & Lake
P.O. Box 4356
San Diego, CA 09876

RE: Your ad for an
Executive Secretary
City Times, 11/20/9X

Dear Ms. Hilman:

Thank you for advertising for an Executive Secretary to work with your top partners. Until I saw your advertisement, I thought no one would appreciate the unusual combination of skills I can offer!

You'll find my resumé enclosed with this letter. Allow me to present the highlights here:

Superior dictaphone skills, steno at 100 words per minute, typing at 60 words per minute on a typewriter, faster with word processing such as ...

... Microsoft Word for Windows, AmiPro and Lotus 1-2-3, all of which I have mastered (along with a basic knowledge of Excel and WordPerfect) through ...

... 4 years at General Electric and 3 years at a Miami-based law firm, specializing in medical malpractice, which accounts for my ...

... professionalism in dealing with the public, attorneys, physicians, emotional clients, and the media ...

... as well as my experience making travel arrangements for overworked lawyers who wish to escape all this!

As an administrative assistant at a smaller firm, I am anxious to assume the additional responsibilities described in your ad. I hope you will contact me for an interview; my address and phone number are printed above. Thank you for considering me.

Sincerely,

Ruth Gorham-Black

Enc: Resumé
        References

Mr. J. Victor Halman
Tedesco Industries Corporation   RE: Office Administrator
9762 South Willens Road   3/12/9X <u>City Times</u>
Columbia, MO 09876   advertisement

Dear Mr. Halman:

To meet the extensive qualifications listed in your advertisement, a candidate must be a true professional with in-depth experience at a major corporation who is looking for an exciting new challenge as I am.

<u>For example, your ad requests:</u>	<u>and I deliver:</u>
Experience screening telephone calls, responding, and routing accordingly	2 years as a receptionist for General American Products
Ability to order, maintain, and distribute office supply inventory	7 years as Office Manager for IBN Executive Offices
Skill in scheduling and coordinating training seminars, meetings, and on-site demonstrations	7 years doing same in addition to coordinating travel arrangements for 15 IBN executives
Knowledge of word processing	WordPerfect, AmiPro, Harvard Graphics

In addition, I possess a degree in Business Administration, exceptional interpersonal and written communication skills. I type at 50 wpm and have easy fluency in Spanish. I would be pleased to take your keyboarding and proofreading tests when we meet for an interview, when I will also detail my salary history and requirements for you.

These qualifications, combined with my substantial experience would make me a productive, effective Office Administrator for Tedesco Industries from my first day on the job. I hope you'll contact me at my home number below; I look forward to meeting you.

Sincerely,

Ashford B. Wells
(555) 765-4321 home telephone

Ms. Teresa Fralisso
Doniger-Davis Management, Inc.
54230 South Ingraham
New Orleans, LA 09876

Dear Ms. Fralisso:

I am writing to explore the possibility of pursuing an Associate's position at Doniger-Davis. Currently, I am a Relationship Officer at American First Bancorporation, where I manage relationships with high net worth individuals. In May 199X, I will earn my MBA in Finance from State University.

My interest in management consulting has been piqued by specific and fascinating classes that are part of the MBA program. Business Policy, Strategic Implementation, and Managing Human Systems, in particular, demonstrated to me that <u>my education, interpersonal talents, and practical experience would prove immensely productive</u> in a consulting environment.

With 5 years in the financial services industry, I can offer your firm <u>a speciality with broad application</u>. My involvement with interviewing and assessing prospective employees and with quality improvement projects may <u>free you from the in-depth training</u> that would be required for a less experienced candidate.

Enclosed is a copy of my resumé for your information. I will call next week to see when we might get together. In the meantime, I thank you for your consideration. I look forward to meeting you.

Sincerely,

Linda Dey Little
(555) 456-7890, extension 98

Ms. Lucille Montana
Montana Consulting
1000 Lakeview Road
Suite 1267
Thunder Lake, MN 09876

Dear Ms. Montana:

I enjoyed speaking with you on the phone this afternoon and appreciate your interest.

As promised, I have enclosed my resumé which details my unusually thorough background in Public Relations, Business Communications and Human Resource Development. What my resumé does not describe is my character. I am a conceptual thinker, a generator of creative ideas, and a self-starter.

I would welcome the opportunity to demonstrate these qualities in person and look forward to hearing from you.

Sincerely,

Cynthia Richards
(555) 765-4321 office
(555) 456-7890 home

Ms. Catherine M. Scully, Vice President
Corporate Communications
SYTEX, Inc.
422 Bethlehem Way
Augusta, GA 09876

Dear Ms. Scully:

Your advertisement for an Events Planner was of particular interest to me because I encounter so few organizations that recognize the unique value of special events. Relegating this function to already overworked marketing departments, where planning withers and presentation suffocates, most firms waste this vital opportunity.

Since SYTEX is not like most firms and I am not like most Events Planners, perhaps we should meet.

I would like to discover more about your events schedule. And I would like to describe my experience designing, planning, preparing, promoting, and running annual meetings, company-wide divisional meetings, regional breakfast meetings, trade shows, and seminars. I have a special expertise in creating events that generate important new business potential while enhancing the corporate image.

In addition, this past year I orchestrated a tour of the Greek Islands for our major shareholders. Not only did this event produce additional stock purchases among our touring group, but through carefully controlled publicity, "less major" stockholders added to their holdings quite significantly as well.

I have enclosed my resumé along with a description of other programs I have designed and the results they have produced. It would be an honor to meet you in person and to be considered as a member of the SYTEX staff.

Sincerely,

Ariadne S. Webb
(555) 765-4321 work
(555) 456-7890 home

Enclosures

Director, Human Resources
Santangelo Resources, Inc.
P.O. Box 1111
Needham, MA 09876

To the Director of Human Resources:

Your recent advertisement in the <u>City Times</u> attracted my attention because I can offer you the precise qualifications you're seeking in a Public Relations Manager.

    Possibly at a lower cost than a more senior executive might demand. But with no less experience.

As you'll see on the enclosed resumé, I currently serve as Associate Public Relations Manager for Columbia Data Systems. Because the company's success depends upon its reputation among a cross section of users, I have worked diligently (and often around the clock) to secure positive publicity for Columbia. In a wide range of media. With a diversity of "stories." Despite decreasing allocations.

Short "statements" add punch!

Of greater significance is that I fought and dispelled the harmful rumors that surfaced as a result of the company's microchip disaster last fall. The crisis management skills I have acquired are critical to any major corporate entity operating under the scrutiny of today's news-hungry media circus.

I am confident that the media contacts, creativity, communication skills, and crisis management abilities I possess will prove invaluable to your firm.

I would welcome the opportunity to meet with you. If you will call or leave a message on my home answering machine, I will return your call promptly.

Sincerely,

Thomas Hoover
(555) 765-4321 daytime

Ms. Susan Stein
Creative Director
Raleigh Advertising
878 Madison Avenue
New York, NY 09876

Dear Ms. Stein:

Having researched your agency and the exceptional results your teams produce, I have identified your firm as one that values creative talent and hard work -- both of which I can deliver.

Although I am certain that you receive hundreds of resumés from people seeking a position with your agency, I urge you to consider mine. The mix of skills I possess differs from those of other graphic designers. For example:

- As a seasoned Art Director/Graphic Designer, I possess extensive corporate experience, working with many of today's leading firms: Met Life, Prudential, IBM, Federal Express, and Sony, among others.

- Well versed in both traditional and computer-aided design and production, I am adept at using Microsoft Word as well as QuarkXPress, Adobe Illustrator, and Adobe Photoshop.

- I have successfully joined forces with clients, management, account, and creative staff to create solutions that work for a range of businesses within a cross section of industries.

With my unique combination of qualifications, you can welcome to your agency a genuine creative talent and true professional -- just as I would welcome the opportunity to meet with you.

I will take the liberty of calling you shortly to see when we might get together.

Sincerely,

Jacqueline DuBois
(555) 456-7890

Mr. Walter LaMotta
Assistant Vice President
UniFirst Savings Bank
100 North Broad Street
Philadelphia, PA 09876

Dear Mr. LaMotta:

GOOD NEWS!

There is a copywriter only a phone call away who knows the difference between a CD, the FDIC, and the SIPC ... one who can express complex details clearly and convincingly to consumers, investors, shareholders.

> **I am an experienced advertising and direct mail copywriter with <u>a strong financial background</u>** -- with the time to put this expertise to work for UniFirst!

You'll add an exceptional member to your marketing team since I've created sales tools, direct mail packages, advertisements, product brochures, and corporate identity pieces quickly and effectively -- <u>often overnight</u>.

Plus, unlike most writers, my background includes staff positions with both advertising agencies and commercial banks. What this means for you is that <u>you'll save hours</u> negotiating with legal counsel, thanks to my in-depth knowledge of government restrictions on financial advertising.

Finally, because I possess such in-depth experience, I am well versed in many financial products and services so I can begin being effective for you <u>immediately</u> without wasting your resources and time on training.

Can I tell you more? If so, you may reach me at (555) 765-4321. In the meantime, I will send samples of my work to your office by messenger within the week.

I thank you in advance for your consideration.

Sincerely,

Jody Lynn Horowitz

Beginning with the creative use of the company's motto, this writer weaves industry lingo into a strong cover letter that resulted in an interview and offer!

AIWA America Inc.
One AIWA Highway
Morristown, NJ 09876

AIWA
I HEAR YA!

Your ad in this Sunday's <u>City Times</u> describes someone who can assist with your sound marketing strategy. My accessories include:

Long Playing Time: Five years marketing and advertising to the audio electronics consumer. For the past 3 years, I've worked with PhonAmerica Audio and Electronics and FFDB Communications to successfully market home and car amps, speakers, receivers, and accessories.

Shock-Resistant Memory: I have followed AIWA's marketing for years and am quite familiar with your product line.

Digital Recording and Playback: Over 7 years' experience with PCs and mainframes; advanced capabilities with WordPerfect and Lotus 1-2-3 spreadsheet construction and analysis.

Heat-Resistant Assembly: I am able to function under pressure at maximum output without fading.

AIWA
I CAN HELP YA!

Please review my attached resumé. I would be happy to discuss salary expectations during a personal interview, for which I can make myself available to fit your schedule.

I look forward to hearing from you.

Sincerely,

Nicholas I. Koenig
Work Telephone: (555) 456-7890
Home Telephone: (555) 765-4321

Same writer, same skills, same use of the company motto as in the previous letter—this time cleverly restated to appeal to a different industry.

Mr. Anthony Lee
NYNEX Mobile Communications
145-65 Fifth Avenue
New York, NY 09876

Dear Mr. Lee:

NYNEX is really going places. And I'd like to come aboard. Not as a passenger, but as a navigator.

Your ad in this Sunday's City Times for an Assistant Advertising Manager intrigues me. I have the skills and experience to help your Advertising Director steer your marketing efforts towards an expanded customer base and increased profits.

You see, through my tenure at two advertising agencies, I've been exposed to every facet of the marketing and advertising process. As I have for Fortune 500 Companies and TelNet, a growing long-distance telecommunications firm, I can help NYNEX develop sound marketing strategies, innovative ad campaigns, targeted direct response programs, and a wealth of original promotional activities.

I would like to bring my knowledge of, and expertise with, many companies to bear for one: NYNEX. And yes, I have the drive to succeed!

Please review my resumé and call me so I can come in for a test drive as soon as possible.

Sincerely,

Nicholas I. Koenig
Work Telephone: (555) 456-7890
Home Telephone: (555) 765-4321

Resumé enclosed

Ms. Marilyn Horning
Vice President
Electronic World, Inc.   RE: Your ad for an
1200 Verdi Way   Account Executive
Venice, CA 09876   City Times, 11/20/9X

Dear Ms. Horning:

Your advertisement caught my eye immediately as it describes a position for which my qualifications are ideal.

My solid experience in sales, marketing, and dealing with both customers and prospects enables you to add a seasoned professional to your team -- one who can begin being productive at once. Allow me to highlight my strengths:

-Nearly 5 years of proven success in selling sophisticated equipment to consumers/the public/corporations/national corporate accounts.

-Highly effective communications skills, which I used to sell a range of electronic products and train customers in using them.

-In-depth experience developing marketing strategies and techniques for use by the sales team.

-Familiarity with, and comfort in, working on a salary plus commission basis.

My resumé provides further details on my background and accomplishments. Realizing that this data cannot adequately convey my personal strengths, I would appreciate the opportunity to meet with you, at which time we could discuss salary in greater depth.

I thank you for your consideration and look forward to hearing from you.

Sincerely,

Michelle S. Neufield
(555) 765-4321

Mr. Theodore Wilson
President
Wilson Manufacturing Corp.
100 Anderson Way
Atlanta, GA 09876

Dear Mr. Wilson:

If you're looking for an exceptional Product Manager
with insight, creativity, a proven record in
Manufacturing and Management, and an impressive work
ethic, look no further.

Through hands-on experience at all levels of
Warehousing, Production, and Sales (detailed in the
enclosed resumé), I have developed superior
analytical and interpersonal skills, marketing
expertise, a perspective and sophistication unique in
our industry -- all of which I can put to work for
you.

I produce an endless supply of new ideas. I can
generate solutions to problems where none seem
possible. And I will teach, inspire, and motivate
others to do the same.

I look forward to speaking with you soon to set up a
convenient time for us to meet. I can be reached at
(555) 765-4321 during the day or evening.

Sincerely,

Charles S. Grentham

Mr. Albert Martinelli
Millerman Fashions
1411 Broadway
New York, NY 09876   **RE:** Product Development

Dear Mr. Martinelli:

The contributions I have made on behalf of my previous employers preview what I can offer Millerman Fashions.

As Associate Product Developer in Ladies Accessories:

- I interact on a daily basis with existing and potential vendors around the world to **initiate, foster, and maintain these key relationships.**

- Researching market trends, I identify those that can be exploited to **bolster product merchandising.**

- I developed a new product line for an important National Account that **reduced inventory overages and increased sales.**

- On the administrative side, I am fully responsible for coordinating sample lines for the National Sales Force and controlling stock levels.

In my previous role as Assistant Showroom Manager:

- I developed new systems and procedures that dramatically **reduced processing errors** on national account sales.

- I served as central liaison for the West Coast region, communicating new product information on a weekly basis.

- I supervised the overall operation of the 6-product-line New York showroom and trained all new associates in showroom maintenance and sales.

In each position, I introduced innovative products and procedures that had direct and positive impact on the company's bottom line profitability -- and I can do the same for Millerman Fashions.

May we have the chance to meet and explore this promising opportunity in greater detail? I will call you shortly.

Sincerely,

Mary Alice Preston
(555) 456-7890 office

Mr. Douglas E. Dixon
World Cruise Lines
867 Park Avenue South
New York, NY 09876

RE: Air/Sea Cruise Product
Development ad
<u>City Times</u> 11/30/9X

Dear Mr. Dixon:

If you are searching for a creative thinker with extensive experience selling to both companies and individuals, we should meet.

I am currently a Vice President in Sales and Marketing at The Ames Company. I am eager to transfer my skills from manufacturing to the travel industry.

-Through delightful cruises in the Caribbean, the Mediterranean, and South America, <u>I have become intimately familiar with the many superb benefits</u> that cruising offers individuals, groups, and corporate planners.

-Through my travels in the Orient, Scandinavia, and Europe, <u>I know first-hand the perspective such exposure affords</u>.

-Through my work with a diverse client base, <u>I have become extremely proficient in promoting high-ticket items</u> by identifying and focusing on the advantages they offer to each member of a varied market.

Because I am currently seeking to broaden my horizons -- literally and figuratively -- I await your reply so that we can arrange a personal meeting. Then, we can discuss how my particular blend of capabilities, experience, and managerial strengths can help your firm capture lucrative business opportunities.

Very truly yours,

Darrell K. Grissolm
Home Telephone: 555-456-7890
Work Telephone: 555-765-4321

This research professional is letting her work speak for her. She's also asked for advice on a resumé—a good way to get it read more carefully.

Mr. Hamilton Green
Green Recruiting, Inc.
Three Broad Hunt Road   RE: Opportunities in
Burlington, VT 09876   Market Research

Dear Mr. Green:

We spoke on Wednesday afternoon and, as promised, here is a copy of my resumé. Since it has been AGES since I've circulated one, I would welcome any suggestions or advice.

I'm also enclosing copies of:

    -Comparative market analyses of male fine apparel purchasers in New York and Chicago, which I conducted for a French clothing retailer.

    -A report I compiled for an organic foods company exploring the efficacy of expanding into the South.

    -A proposal for a focus group to help a major airline assess the popularity of new routes and frequent flyer program enhancements.

Call me whenever you like with questions. I can be reached at either phone number this weekend. (I work from home.) My work number is also an automatic fax.

Sincerely,

Martha C. Tchetynkya
(555) 456-7890 Home
(555) 765-4321 Work/Fax

Ms. Debora Crain
President
Crain Employment Agency   RE: Opportunities in
Fort Collins, CO 09876   Product Management

Dear Ms. Crain:

Your work and reputation within the advertising/marketing industry suggest that you continually update your roster of highly qualified executives to fill positions on both the agency and the client side of the business.

Good opening in letter to recruiter

For this reason, I am writing to introduce myself: a marketing pro who has spent the last 10 years promoting a cross section of consumer and business-to-business services. My work at the Holmes & Richards advertising agency has equipped me with the following skills, all of which are essential to an effective Product Manager:

-The promotional perspective produced by a decade-long career on the agency side of the business, now complemented by a desire to join the client side.

-The ability to master complex product details and identify related benefits for each of several diverse target market segments.

-The communication and presentation skills critical to articulating these benefits clearly and accurately to co-workers, sales representatives, creative staff, senior management, and prospective customers.

Each of these qualities is integral to the Product Manager who will build sales and profits for her agency and its client. Combined, they produce a proven professional with the experience and creativity to explore and exploit every opportunity for growth.

In your clients' searches for managers to champion their companies' products, why not recommend a proven marketing expert like myself? Because I would welcome the opportunity to meet you, I will call early next week to see if we might get together.

Thank you in advance for your consideration.

Sincerely,

Erica Hamilton-Brown
(555) 765-4321

Enc: Resumé

Ms. Elizabeth DeMario
Mr. Jake Williams
DeMario & Williams Advertising
143 Congress Street
Baltimore, MD 09876

Dear Ms. DeMario and Mr. Williams:

Welcome to Baltimore!

The West Coast's loss is our gain. With nontraditional marketing
avenues rapidly expanding, these promise to be exciting times for those
prepared to identify and creatively exploit new opportunities in new
markets …

… <u>as DeMario & Williams does. As I do.</u>

Enclosed, therefore, is my resumé and more: the profile of a successful
marketing pro who has produced, literally, **tens of millions** of dollars in
the last ten years … who has **experience with agencies and clients of
all sizes and specialties** … who has **developed** business where none
appeared to exist … who is **creative, self-motivated,** and **hungry** for a
new challenge.

Because I've worked in New York, Philadelphia, and Baltimore (my
home town), I can offer DeMario & Williams an intimate perspective of
East Coast thought processes, likes and dislikes, and the hot buttons that
must be pushed to get things done.

I would welcome the opportunity to demonstrate my strengths and
talents in person and look forward to hearing from you.

Sincerely,

I. Claire Reston
(555) 456-7890

Director, Human Resources
DGM Corporation   RE: 1/7/9X <u>City Times</u> ad
P.O. Box 1111   Senior Marketing Associate
Vienna, VA 09876

To the Director of Human Resources:

Timely opening

Happy New Year! Throughout my 8 years in marketing, the start of a new year invariably produced fresh ideas and renewed excitement for launching marketing initiatives -- and now I can offer your firm a new perspective, as well.

With the rapid evolution of the financial services industry, my role as a marketing and advertising manager exposed me to a range of promotional challenges previously unknown in banking. I mastered the ability to identify and quantify objectives, refine them in response to market research and develop detailed plans and budgets. I learned to think in entirely new ways, to motivate creative talent and produce campaigns, promotions, and individual sales pieces that added significantly to my employer's bottom line.

These are the skills that define the successful Senior Marketing Associate in any industry. I offer them to your firm -- along with my in-depth experience in strategic planning for retail, commercial, and business-to-business advertising.

I look forward to hearing from you.

Sincerely,

Anita Sharfin
(555) 456-7890

Mr. Abraham D. Kingford
President, CEO
King Information Systems
765 Rumson Road
Medford, NJ 09876

RE: Your ad for a
Senior National Sales Consultant
<u>City Times</u>, 11/20/9X

Dear Mr. Kingford:

Promises benefits right up front.

As the current top biller for a major publisher of electronic reference information products, I am writing to you because I am eager to expand from a regional sales territory to the national level -- and can deliver several advantages that my peers may not offer you.

Eight years in sales and electronic technologies have equipped me with the following unique capabilities:

Strategy development and implementation: to promote electronic products and services to over 125 major academic institutions and businesses throughout the Northeast.

Proven ability to initiate, maintain, and build ongoing relationships with key accounts in academia and corporate markets: to help maximize opportunities for revenue growth.

Exceptional expertise in a full range of electronic reference media including CD ROM, multimedia, online, and diverse electronic database applications.

In addition, I am able to work effectively and independently in the field without requiring costly, time-consuming supervision. Perhaps most importantly, I have developed <u>strong presentation and sales closing skills</u> that I can put to work immediately with the <u>solid base of contacts</u> I will bring to your organization.

My resumé, which is enclosed, details my career, accomplishments and my education (BA in Economics/MBA.) Currently, my total compensation approaches six figures including base salary, commissions, bonuses, and expenses. I would be pleased to discuss my qualifications and salary/commission requirements in greater detail when we meet in person.

Because I operate from the field, please leave a message for me at (555) 456-7890 and I will contact you at once to schedule a meeting.

Sincerely,

K. Stuart Linnahan
(555) 456-7890

This writer's impressive accomplishments warrant a lengthy letter. Note how the writer skillfully breaks the first page in the middle of a compelling statement to encourage the reader to turn to the second page.

Mr. Joseph Runnell, Senior Vice President
Boston First Financial Corporation
1343 Boyleston Street
Boston, MA 09876

Dear Mr. Runnell:

With the financial services industry breaking new ground every day, there is no time to waste in your search for a Director of Corporate Marketing. So I won't waste yours.

I am a Strategic Marketing Planning/Program Manager with 20+ years experience in services marketing -- the most recent 8 years in telecommunications and, prior to that, in international transportation.

As head of Marketing Services for The New England Telephone Company, I function as an internal Marketing Consultant to the organization's Strategic Business Units -- managing a staff of 14 marketing professionals and a $2MM annual marketing budget, coordinating all advertising, research, direct mail and sales management initiatives.

Marketing program improvements that I introduced raised the visibility of the organization and its products while simultaneously trimming Marketing Department overhead by 50%.

Complementing my broad marketing background is my experience as Controller at an $80MM division of TransInternational Airlines, at that time a $2 billion, Fortune 500 international transportation company. In addition to macro production-revenue forecasting, I directed complete product costing/pricing and overall government regulatory agency (CAB) financial reporting and compliance.

Advances I introduced at TransInternational significantly enhanced the competitiveness of the airline's product and, in the

(please turn)

98

(continued)

process, I became a recognized expert in airline operations and economics, demonstrating the depth of my commitment to product.

The success of my marketing programs during the last dozen years is directly attributable to several unique talents I can offer Boston First:

- I leverage my strategic planning skills to successfully convert Management's business plans into achievable marketing initiatives.

- I maximize my financial controls experience to ensure that those same marketing programs are firmly grounded in economic reality.

- I creatively empower subordinates with increasing program management responsibilities.

- Through strict adherence to a process of Total Quality Management, I guarantee that all marketing programs managed by my department are completed <u>on time, within budget, to the client's satisfaction</u>.

These are the proven achievements and talents I can bring to Boston First. Let's get together to discuss this opportunity in greater detail. I can be reached during the day at (555) 456-7890 or in the evening at (555) 765-4321.

Sincerely,

Arthur L. Lewis

Knowing that a recruiter would need only an overview of the key points contained in the previous letter, this executive successfully edited it to create the letter shown on this page.

Ms. Nora L. McGuigon
D.B. Ennis Associates
958 Jefferson Avenue
Boston, MA 09876

Dear Ms. McGuigon:

What a pleasure speaking with you this morning about my job search! As promised, I have enclosed my resumé so that you and your associates may keep me in mind should an appropriate situation surface. To preview the information enumerated on my resumé, let me summarize my background and strengths for you:

I am a Strategic Marketing Planning/Program Manager with 20+ years experience in services marketing -- the most recent 8 years in telecommunications and, prior to that, in international transportation.

As head of Marketing Services for The New England Telephone Company, I function as an internal Marketing Consultant to the organization's Strategic Business Units -- managing a staff of 14 marketing professionals and a $2MM annual marketing budget, coordinating all advertising, research, direct mail and sales management initiatives.

Marketing program improvements that I introduced raised the visibility of the organization and its products while simultaneously trimming Marketing Department overhead by 50%.

Complementing my broad marketing background is my experience as Controller at an $80MM division of TransInternational Airlines, at that time a $2 billion, Fortune 500 international transportation company. In addition to macro production-revenue forecasting, I directed complete product costing/pricing and overall government regulatory agency (CAB) financial reporting and compliance.

Advances I introduced at TransInternational significantly enhanced the competitiveness of the airline's product and, in the

(please turn)

(continued)

process, I became a recognized expert in airline operations and economics, demonstrating the depth of my commitment to product.

Having recently engineered the downsizing of our business-to-business Marketing Services area, I am now anxious to apply my marketing communications expertise to situations in which the pace of growth and opportunity represents more of a challenge. If you see a match between your clients' needs and my experience, I would welcome the opportunity for further discussion.

I can be reached during the day at (555) 456-7890 or in the evening at (555) 765-4321. In the meantime, I will, of course, let you know of any change in my employment situation.

Sincerely,

Arthur L. Lewis

Enclosure

Mr. Robert McCarthy
Director, Customer Service
Edison Electric
7600 Wilshire Boulevard
Irvine, CA 09876

Dear Mr. McCarthy:

It is tempting to telephone in response to your ad for a Customer Service Representative since the majority of service transactions take place over the phone these days.

Instead, I enclose my resumé as you requested, providing you with in-depth information on the 11 years I have spent dealing with the public. Throughout this time, I have successfully resolved customer claims and accurately recorded complex product orders with consistent praise from my supervisors.

More importantly, I have enhanced each company's reputation, keeping existing customers satisfied and transforming first-time buyers into loyal, repeat purchasers.

I would appreciate the chance to do the same for your organization and will call you shortly so that you can experience my skills on a first-hand basis.

Sincerely,

Jeannette Flavio
555-456-0789 (evenings)

Here's an effective way to turn a negative into a positive. This jobhunter has held a string of jobs, but discusses this openly as a benefit to the reader.

Sales Manager
<u>The Yellow Pages</u>   RE: Your <u>City Times</u>
P.O. Box 1111   ad for a Sales Rep
Lansing, MI 09876

To the Sales Manager:

I suspect you'll find very few candidates with a background such as mine -- and it's one I'd like to put to work on your behalf.

As you'll see on the enclosed resumé, the <u>depth of my experience</u> in sales offers you the opportunity to hire a real pro who needs little or no training and who is comfortable and successful with cold canvassing.

Moreover, having worked as a Sales Representative in a variety of industries, I have the background to construct sales pitches meaningful to the variety of different businesses that advertise in *The Yellow Pages* … to turn interest into revenue for you. It is only due to the long-term economic volatility (resulting in downsizing, layoffs, mergers, and business failures) that I have held positions at numerous companies. However, it is this fact that allows me to offer you such an unusual <u>breadth of experience</u>.

A personal interview would allow me to demonstrate my talents. I look forward to hearing from you so that we can schedule a meeting.

Sincerely,

Reed L. Larson
(555) 765-4321

A focused, well written letter such as this can put those of more experienced candidates to shame.

Ms. Dorothy Gilbert Andresen
Blooming Brides   RE: Your ad for
18 Main Street   a Sales Consultant
Greenwich, CT 09876   <u>City Times</u>, 11/20/9X

Dear Ms. Andresen:

In presenting myself as a candidate for the position of Sales Consultant, I present you with a valuable opportunity:

> **To hire an experienced, accomplished expert who can simultaneously handle demanding, often stressed clientele with kid gloves.**

Having planned weddings for my own daughters, I am adept at dealing with the multifaceted stress of the wedding gown selection and fitting process. Patiently, I assessed the virtues of lace, organza, tulle, and silk -- the covered or off-the-shoulder design -- knee, calf, or floor lengths. Gracefully, I balanced my daughters' concerns with those of their friends, husbands-to-be, even mothers-in-law. Delicately, I increased our maximum budget as warranted to include all essential accessories. Conscientiously, I maintained our selection and fitting schedule. Unbelievably, I enjoyed it immensely -- all four times!

Through it all, I was amazed to discover that my hands-on experience proved consistently more effective than that of our sales representatives, which is why I offer myself as a candidate.

After some time at home, I am now rejoining the work force. I would welcome the opportunity to meet with you. Please give me a call at (555) 456-7890 day or evening so that we can schedule an appointment.

Sincerely,

Bea Bruner

Mr. Rolando Eden
Godiva Chocolates
152 Fifth Avenue
New York, NY 09876

Dear Mr. Eden:

I simply cannot resist responding to your ad for a Sales Representative!

Solid sales experience is only the first of my qualifications -- I have a successful track record and the recommendations to back it up.

Proven ability to translate consumer desires into purchase decisions is only the second of my qualifications -- I have sold effectively within religious, upscale, and ethnic markets.

Superior customer service delivery is only the third qualification I possess -- I project warmth, enthusiasm, and a pleasant attitude.

Above all and unlike almost everyone in the world, I love chocolate but can resist the temptation to sample the inventory!

Combined, these qualifications make me a prime candidate for your sales position. I hope you'll contact me for a personal interview. I can be reached at (555) 456-7890 during the day and at (555) 765-4321 during the evening.

Sincerely,

Riley B. Kruger, Jr.

Enclosed: Resumé

*Clever way
to
get attention*

Mr. Andrew Hoffman
Town and Country Home
84 Manning Way
Evanston, IL 09876

Dear Mr. Hoffman:

If your advertisement in the <u>City Times</u> was written to attract my attention, it worked like a charm!

As the enclosed resumé demonstrates, my background, experience, and proven accomplishments combine to make me the ideal Senior Buyer for Town and Country Home.

I have held a variety of positions in retail management with a particular emphasis in buying, having served as **a Buyer for B. Altman & Co. with responsibility for purchasing in both domestic and international markets.** In this position, I acquired a profound understanding of the unique preferences of the upscale consumer, which could help you avoid costly experiments (not to mention embarrassing failures) with this demanding market segment.

My current involvement in the direction of the **development of innovative consumer product lines** will also be of value to you. I have been personally instrumental in engineering successful promotional programs that produced annual sales well over **$3 million** each.

Although I am secure in my current position, I realize that future growth may be limited. The opportunity to lend my expertise to Town and Country Home would be an exciting one. I hope you will give me a call so that we may schedule a convenient time to meet. Your discretion in contacting me is most appreciated.

Sincerely,

Vivan L. Steers
(555) 456-7890 work telephone
(555) 765-4321 answering service

Mr. Lionel Adams, President
Surplus Warehouse, Inc.
230 Crossways Boulevard
Tulsa, OK 09876

Dear Mr. Adams:

As Vice President of Retail Operations for a nationwide office supply chain, I reduced operating expenditures by more than $2 million last year. I further developed tightened security measures accounting for a 50% reduction in losses due to employee and customer theft.

Proven results such as these are critical to your firm's ongoing profitability -- and they are precisely what I can bring to Surplus Warehouse.

Having engineered the planning and launch of 54 retail locations across the country, which generated an additional $350 million in sales, I can direct your company in its ongoing expansion efforts with ease and expertise.

These are only two chapters in a career story that spans 24 years in retailing. Additional successes, innovations, and cost saving stories are detailed on the enclosed resumé.

Let's get together so that I can demonstrate the advantages my experience can offer Surplus Warehouse.

Sincerely,

H. Michael Gorman, III
(555) 456-7890

Ms. Laurel Simone
President
Inroads Automotive
230 Crossways Boulevard
Fresno, CA 09876

Dear Ms. Simone:

Over the years, I have been well aware of Inroads Automotive's continuing success.

As a customer and fellow member of the retailing profession, I have been impressed with the way your company stays ahead of your competition -- by correctly predicting in advance what products and services the public will demand, and then delivering them.

This is exactly how I direct my professional career, which leads me to send you my resumé now.

> **By carefully monitoring sales and industry trends, I significantly improved inventory management, increasing sales and broadening our customer base.**

> **I have also adapted MIS programs in conjunction with merchants to streamline inventory controls and reporting procedures without increasing expenses.**

In your search for a Distribution Manager, I hope you will consider me a serious candidate. When we meet, I will be pleased to provide information on my salary history as well as recommendations from previous employers.

I look forward to hearing from you.

Sincerely,

Dorothy Bridle
(555) 456-7890

Ms. Amelia Trost
Director, Human Resources
Grenville Manufacturing, Inc.
86 Anthrax Way
Burlington, NJ 09876

RE: City Times 7/19/9X ad for
      Senior Subcontracts Administrator

Dear Ms. Trost:

The position described in your advertisement is the job I have been preparing for throughout my career.

> -Having worked as both an Assistant Procurement Manager and a Subcontracts Administrator for a major equipment manufacturer, I have mastered the tactics required to successfully select, bid out, negotiate with, and manage independent vendors.

> -From my first day on the job, I will skillfully evaluate proposals, analyze risks, conduct contract negotiations, and perform cost analyses for you.

> -I have handled in excess of 300 individual purchase orders simultaneously -- some worth over $100 million each.

> -Most importantly, I have negotiated savings up to 30% on new procurements.

As the enclosed resumé attests, my experience is proven, the results measurable and substantial.

I would like to meet with you to further demonstrate my abilities. Please contact me at home at (555) 765-4321 as my current employer is not aware of my desire to join another company.

Sincerely,

Lisa Quimby

Mr. Frederick List
The Randolph Chemical Company
765 North Winter Street
Randolph, AZ 09876

RE: *City Times* 5/20/9X ad for an
Accounts Receivable Coordinator

Dear Mr. List:

Tact. Diplomacy. Presence. The traits most critical to success in collections are also the most difficult to find. I am pleased to offer you these indispensable skills -- and more:

-5 years of experience in receivables billing, data entry, cash receipts entry and processing, cash collection reporting

-Expertise in systems and telephone support

-Solid third-party billing and collections experience

-Mastery of WordPerfect and Lotus 1-2-3

-Superior organizational and communication skills

When we meet you'll discover that, in hiring me, you immediately secure a professional who can work productively with your Account Executives to monitor past-due receivables and handle sensitive situations with firmness and delicacy. To support a productive team effort, not build an empire.

If you'll contact me at (555) 765-4321, we can schedule an interview to discuss my salary history in detail as well as this exciting opportunity.

Sincerely,

Franz Manheim
(555) 765-4321

Ms. Myra Richards
Financial Division
United Recruiting Corporation
P.O. Box 182
New York, NY 09876

RE: Your advertisement for a
Financial Analyst in the
<u>New York Times</u>
January 12, 199X

Dear Ms. Richards:

Are you searching for someone with a <u>thorough understanding</u> of the principles that support the operation of today's financial institutions and capital markets? Someone with the <u>ability</u> and <u>enthusiasm</u> to critically participate in investment decisions? Someone who is upbeat, positive, learns quickly and who is <u>not afraid of hard work</u>?

If so, we should meet. As a graduate student at the University of Pennsylvania specializing in financial and international business, I expect to complete my MBA in May of this year. My goal is to put my <u>strong academic background in finance</u> to use in the world of business.

Throughout my graduate studies, I have focused on money and banking, international trade finance, and portfolio management. More specifically, I have conducted in-depth research on issues relating to:

- The functions of the central banks and their effects on the world economies.

- The operations of the world market and foreign exchange, as well as their impact on the U.S. economy.

- The underlying models of portfolio analysis such as the capital asset pricing model and arbitrage pricing theory.

My resumé, which is enclosed, further details my qualifications. I look forward to meeting with you to discuss how I can contribute to your company's bottom line.

I thank you in advance for your time and consideration.

Sincerely,

Thomas Frank

Ms. Sherry Sites
Steckler Financial, Inc.
1357 Morning Street
Winston, NC 09876

Dear Ms. Sites:

Ralph Enwood suggested I contact you regarding the current opening in
your brokerage division. With my MBA firmly in hand this coming July
and several years of real world experience, I would welcome the
opportunity to contribute to the success your firm already enjoys.

I have enclosed my resumé to supply specific information on my
background. Allow me to provide you with the highlights:

- As a manager of finance for a discount brokerage group, I
  gained a profound understanding of the constant demands a
  consumer customer base makes on traders and support staff --
  and how to meet these demands.

- I earned my Series 7 and Series 63 licenses while working full
  time -- a sound illustration of my work ethic and ability to
  complete simultaneous, challenging projects.

- I have been regularly praised by my superiors and professors
  for my written and verbal communication skills. I work well
  with others and enjoy assuming additional responsibility.

I would very much like to meet with you to explore your operations and
the possibility of employment. The opportunity to join a winning team
such as yours -- and add to its success -- is one I would relish.

Sincerely,

Rita Lenghorn
(555) 456-7890

cc: Ralph Enwood

Mr. Joachim J. Manengues
Senior Vice President
Dallas First Bancorporation
987 North Diversity Drive
Dallas, TX 09876

> RE: <u>City Times</u> 6/2/9X ad for a
> Cash Management Sales Officer

Dear Mr. Manengues:

Six years of solid, in-depth banking experience. Expertise in handling commercial relationships with businesses earning up to $50 million in sales. A commitment to new business development. This is what I can bring to Dallas First Bancorporation, at once.

As an Assistant Vice President in Private Banking with Dallas Bancshares, I earned my MBA in Finance from State University, and I am looking to transfer my financial and business development talents from private to corporate banking.

Dealing with a diverse client list -- small to medium-sized companies, top executives of leading corporations, accomplished (and demanding!) entertainers -- I am adept at identifying cash management opportunities and providing solutions to short- and long-term cash flow needs for corporate clients.

As requested in your ad, I am faxing you my resumé. My current compensation includes base salary and commissions, and ranges from $60,000 to $80,000 annually. I am anxious to set up a meeting with you to discuss in greater detail your position and my unique qualifications. I will call you later in the day, or you may contact me at work at (555) 123-4567.

I look forward to speaking with you.

Sincerely,

Burton M. Migynsum

Mr. Alfred Masoni
Vice President, Private Banking
All City National Bank
123 Avon Road
Los Angeles, CA 09876

Dear Mr. Masoni:

The enclosed resumé details my achievements as an experienced private banker. However, it cannot demonstrate the maturity, insight, and new business development finesse I have acquired. These are the qualities I would like to show you first-hand.

Because I have worked closely with customers at every level -- platform and private, retail and commercial -- I have developed superior interpersonal skills, broad product knowledge, a sure grasp of financial strategies and risk tolerance.

States skills gained— not work history.

I can track down new business opportunities in an adverse economy. I can work effectively on my own while contributing fresh ideas to the team. I can learn from and support my co-workers with an attitude that is positive and pleasant.

May I demonstrate to you the advantages my experience can offer you? I will telephone your office early next week to see when we might meet.

Sincerely,

Mary Royce
(555) 456-7890 home
(555) 765-4321 office

Mr. Andrew U. Harris
Newman Personnel, Inc.   RE: Your ad for a Lending Officer
9200 Fifth Avenue   City Times 5/2/9X
Wilmington, DE 09876

Dear Mr. Harris:

I had the pleasure of speaking with you several years ago and I thought I would write to you now in response to your recent ad for a Lending Officer.

Since we last spoke, I have expanded my career in financial services and am now ideally qualified to function as a superior Lending Officer. In addition to 7 years of valuable banking experience, a BA in Economics and an MBA, I can offer your clients strong capabilities, including, among others:

-Expertise in handling relationships up to and exceeding $50 million in size.

-A history of achieving account profitability while ensuring client confidence and satisfaction.

-Mastery of analysis and recommendation for substantial commercial and personal loans.

I have enclosed an updated resumé that details my training, professional experience and accomplishments. If you would call, with discretion, at (555) 456-7890, I would be happy to meet with you or anyone you might recommend.

I thank you in advance for any assistance you may provide.

Sincerely,

L. Gavin Kramer

Mr. Rupert Anceleri
Prime First Bancorporation
1234 Main Street
Evansville, IN 09876

Dear Mr. Anceleri:

After working successfully for 20 years on a consultancy basis, I am now searching for a different challenge. Your organization came immediately to mind due to its reputation as a leading lender to entrepreneurial firms across the country.

The depth of experience I can offer would prove indispensable in your efforts to identify sound, solid growth firms. I have worked with a broad range of companies including: manufacturing businesses such as fabrication, assembly, and foundry companies; distributors of commodity and value-added products; importers of both hard and soft goods and service companies in a variety of industries.

My in-depth experience with entrepreneurs and with companies whose annual sales range from $1 million to $50 million positions me to identify and assess the potential of growing firms with skilled management and promising customer sales. I have handled highly leveraged transactions, recapitalizations of LBO financings, turnarounds, workouts, bridge financings, and DIP credit facilities.

Moreover, I have established long-term relationships with attorneys and accountants who have referred clients to me and will continue to do so.

I would welcome the opportunity to discuss with you the numerous benefits my background could provide to Prime First. Let's get together to explore the possibilities. I will contact you to schedule an appointment.

Looking forward to meeting you, I am,

Willam Robertson Fromm
(555) 456-7890

Director of Recruitment
The Monsanto Company
2400 Olive Street Road
St. Louis, MO 09876

RE: Your ad in the Fall issue of
<u>Chemical Engineer</u> for a
Research Director.

Dear Recruitment Director:

In your ad, you list five specific qualifications you seek in a Research Director to join your company. My background and experience enable me to meet each of your requirements and then some.

For example, **you seek** …

and I deliver …

Fertilization production experience	Four years with Dow Chemical's soil enhancement division.
Management experience	Supervised staff of 20 researchers in pursuit of water-soluble environmentally safe microcatalyst.
Proven track record in research	Directed this team to successfully identify what is now the leading microcatalyst in use on American farms.
8 years experience	10 years research, Dow Chemical 4 years teaching, Cal Tech
BSCE Degree	BSCE Degree, Johns Hopkins University

In addition, my teaching experience proved instrumental in presenting this new technology to government officials in order to secure government approval. I also served as liaison with the press to ensure correct introduction of the new product information.

As you can see, my strengths fit your requirements quite well. I would like to discuss my background with you in a personal meeting, at which time I would be happy to detail my salary history and expectations.

I can be reached at (555) 654-3210 during the daytime and (555) 345-4567 in the evening. I look forward to hearing from you.

Sincerely,

Mary Beth Roberts

International correspondence requires a more formal tone, which this writer has used.

Mr. William Ancyle
Senior Program Officer, Water Resources
World Coalition Environment Program
Box 34567
Dakar, Senegal

Dear Mr. Ancyle:

I am writing to you at the recommendation of Madame Eugenie Enchant, Chief of the World Coalition Environment Program Regional Office, who suggested my unusual qualifications might be valuable to WCEP's water resource projects. I will be relocating to Tokyo, Japan in May of 199X to complete my Master's Degree in Environmental Engineering, and I hope to join a project such as yours in September of that year.

My unique background, technical expertise, language abilities, and skill at coordinating multifaceted projects allow me to offer meaningful benefits to your project teams. After 13 years in the environmental field, as detailed on the enclosed resumé, I have mastered the preparation of technical water resource engineering analyses, community and regional planning reports, and comprehensive environmental impact studies. In addition, I can successfully manage complex engineering and planning projects and direct the positive, constructive interaction of the general public, clients, and government agencies.

I am comfortable working and living in international settings, having spent a portion of my childhood in Europe, studied abroad, and completed internships in Japan and Morocco. I am fluent in English, French, and Japanese.

I would like to explore opportunities to apply my professional experience in environmental engineering. I am particularly interested in the WCEP water resource protection and development programs in Africa, the Plan of Action for the Nogbutu River, the desertification work for the Kalahari and the Global Environment Facility.

To this end, I will telephone within the next two weeks to pursue any avenues you might recommend. Meanwhile, please feel free to contact me by fax or letter regarding how I might contribute to the World Coalition's Environment Program.

Sincerely,

Christopher H. Mitori
14 Ellsworth Street
Annandale, VA 09876 USA
(555) 456-7890: home telephone

cc: Madame Enchant, WCEP Paris

Ms. Dorothy Liu
Director, Human Resources
AdvantAmerica Corporation
Ten Commerce Square
Jacksonville, FL 09876

Dear Ms. Liu:

In a large corporation such as yours, the potential for employee misconduct is great. As you know, improprieties can have far-reaching consequences -- for the company's performance, its credibility, and its other staff members.

<u>I can help you avoid such troubling circumstances through my ability to identify employee misconduct and then handle it according to proper legal procedures ... yet with discretion.</u>

My experience as a DEA Special Agent and Inspector General for the City's Housing Department is **unique among my peers.** These jobs have equipped me to **handle a variety of investigations,** including surveillance of employee time abuse, malfeasance, bribery, theft, improper reporting of sick leave, drinking violations, and others. My preparation for, and **participation in, hearings at the state and local level** will serve you well in those rare instances where litigation is necessary.

Hiring a proven professional like myself can save you time, money, and all of the headaches associated with negative publicity. I will contact you next week to see when we might schedule an appointment.

I look forward to meeting you.

Sincerely,

Kelly Marie Blair
(555) 456-7890

Mr. William Robinson
President
Robinson Private Security, Inc.
8200 Georgia Avenue
Atlanta, GA 09876

Dear Mr. Robinson:

With fewer resources upon which to draw, Security Officers working in the private sector frequently assume more varied and challenging responsibilities than many city police officers working as a team.

It's essential, therefore, that the private Security Officer you hire possess in-depth experience, broad-based training, and the proven ability to perform in difficult, dangerous situations. A quick scan of this list of my abilities will prove that I am this officer:

-Undercover investigations

-Financial audits to identify drug-oriented profits; court-qualified expert in deciphering narcotics ledgers

-Coordination of complex, interagency investigations

-Evidence handling and testimony

-Asset forfeiture investigations at state and federal level

-Adherence to policy and procedure

-National jurisdiction for drug-related offenses

-Licensed for weapons use

You'll find supplementary information on my resumé, which is enclosed. I would like to further prove my abilities to you in a personal meeting, when we could discuss my salary history and requirements.

I hope to hear from you.

Sincerely,

Ingmar Johannson
(555) 456-7890 work

Mr. Hank Felipe
Felipe Construction
65 Pershing Street
Helena, MT 09876

Dear Mr. Felipe:

After 6 years in construction, there is no doubt that this is where my skills and interest lie.

My resumé (enclosed) describes the extensive range of projects on which I've worked, both commercial and residential. Throughout, I have received consistent praise from my superiors and have enjoyed the ongoing support of co-workers, many of whom have offered to serve as references for me.

The pressures of the current economic downturn have forced my current employer to reduce his full-time staff. For this reason, I would welcome the opportunity to interview for a position at Felipe Construction.

I can be reached at (555) 456-7890.

Sincerely,

John Noonan

Mr. Allen G. Pearlstine
Pearlstine Management Corp.   RE: Your ad for a
42 Riverview Plaza   Superintendent
Memphis, TN 09876   <u>City Times</u>, 11/20/9X

Dear Mr. Pearlstine:

Eleven years of hands-on experience as a building superintendent has
made me more qualified than many others who may respond to your ad.
The enclosed resumé details my strengths; here is an overview:

   -Experienced with both residential and commercial buildings

   -Ability to supervise in-house maintenance staff, outside
   vendors, and interact effectively with tenants

   -Proficient in all aspects of maintenance including plumbing
   and carpentry

   -Valid #6 Oil, Standpipe and Sprinkler System Licenses

   -Knowledgeable in tool inventory control, supply requisition

   -Fluent in English and Spanish

As you can see, I possess solid, practical experience that I can put to
use for you right away, as my present employer is relocating its
headquarters out of state.

You can reach me at the address and phone numbers listed above. I look
forward to hearing from you.

Sincerely,

Roy L. Harmon

This succinct summary worked well in response to an ad that was impossibly vague.

Mr. Bart J. Crown
Crown Management Corp.   RE: 1/23/9X <u>City Times</u> ad
1818 Crown Plaza   Real Estate Facilities
Kansas City, MO 09876   and Construction

Dear Mr. Crown:

I am writing to schedule a time for us to discuss the position mentioned in your ad. My background in real estate has equipped with me exceptional practical skills and an in-depth understanding of our industry. I would welcome the chance to explore how my strengths might contribute to the success of your firm.

Presently, I am involved in real estate as an owner, landlord, and building superintendent. As a result, I am intimately familiar with legal regulations, housing requirements, construction, electrical, and plumbing. I am licensed in this state as a building inspector, EPA-Certified Radon Technician and Pest Control Inspector. I am also working toward a Masters Degree in Real Estate at State University.

Because I am eager to explore the possibility of working with your firm, I will call you next week to see when we might meet. Or you can reach me at (555) 765-4321.

Sincerely,

Louis H. Kozinsky

Enclosed: Resumé

Ms. Rachel Bell
American Service Corporation
1234 Main Street
Milwaukee, WI 09876

Dear Ms. Bell:

The speed and frequency with which today's organizations relocate, expand, and contract has placed corporate real estate under increasing scrutiny. As a result, the relationship between real estate and overall strategic planning has become more critical than ever.

Only a seasoned real estate professional like myself can accurately balance the impact of real estate assets on your firm's business and financial strategy, profitability, and risk mitigation.

For more than 25 years, I have represented public and private sector clients in every aspect of the real estate transaction. I am now ready to offer my expertise to a company such as yours on a full-time basis.

Having worked in every major market, I can identify the properties that best meet your needs and negotiate optimal terms on your behalf. I have proven skill in dealing effectively with real estate experts, architects, space planners, construction estimators, financial analysts, and lawyers to streamline the planning process.

I will contact you shortly to explore the advantages my experience can offer your organization.

Sincerely,

Gordon H. Bork
(555) 456-7890

Mr. Roger Rossi, President
Rossi Associates
Suite 300
4901 Andrews Road
Seattle, WA 09876

Dear Mr. Rossi:

I am responding to your advertisement for a Senior Architect for two reasons.

<u>Firstly, I can deliver precisely the attributes, experience, and background you seek in a Senior Architect.</u> As you'll see on the enclosed resumé, I have a strong background in commercial interiors and retail design, honed through 12 years with a major New York-based commercial firm.

In my current position, I assume all of the responsibilities typically demanded of a Senior Architect, including:

-Preparation of architectural plans, drawings, and specifications

-Construction and contract administration

-Review of design, code, and construction drawings

-Supervision of construction contractors, contract administration

-Project management through all project phases including programming, planning, design, and construction contract administration

My conceptual abilities are outstanding, my approach consistently team-oriented and I am an AutoCAD wizard! I earned my BA in Architectural Design from the State University Design School. <u>These strengths, along with my clear knowledge of building architectural systems, construction procedures and practices will allow me to add value to your firm at once.</u>

Secondly, I will be relocating to the Seattle area (and am in the process of obtaining Washington State Licensure.) It would be a privilege to meet with you personally to discuss the opportunity to add to your team. I will follow up by calling you soon to schedule an appointment.

Sincerely,

Lynn Beacon

Mr. Ron Bradley
Redmond Communications
P.O. Box 1111
Altaverde, CA 09876

RE: 5/15/9X <u>City Times</u> ad for Word Processors

Dear Mr. Bradley:

It would be a pleasure to meet with you so that I might demonstrate how my abilities fit your needs precisely.

As you'll see on the enclosed resumé, I am proficient in a variety of word processing programs as well as stenography. I am experienced in handling general office duties and answering phones cordially and courteously.

What my resumé does not reveal is my professional demeanor and appearance. In a business environment, these qualities are of the utmost importance in dealing with clients as well as co-workers. In me, you'll discover a reliable, detail-oriented and extremely hard-working associate -- one who will serve as a model to encourage other staff members to demonstrate the same high standard of professionalism.

If you will contact me at (555) 456-7890, we can schedule an appointment.

Sincerely,

Aqueelah Johnson
(555) 456-7890

Mr. Sheldon Ballou
Imprint Publishing
19 Greene Street
New York, NY 09876

RE: 5/15/9X <u>City Times</u>
ad for Word Processors

Dear Mr. Ballou:

Why waste another minute of your valuable time -- time that could be
spent more productively if you had reliable, expert word processing
support? Now that you have my resumé in your hands (see attached),
you can end your search.

> I am an exceptional typist (85 wpm) and can work in
> Microsoft Word, Quattro, WordPerfect 5.1, 5.2 and 6.0 with
> my eyes shut!

I would be pleased to handle the additional responsibilities of
stenography, answering telephones, training others in word processing,
etc. Plus, I am bilingual (English/Chinese), which may strengthen the
service you provide to Asian customers.

You can reach me at (555) 456-7890 during the day and at (555) 765-4321
after business hours. I hope to hear from you.

Sincerely,

Gwendolyn Ellys
(555) 456-7890

Ms. Diane Sweet
ArbiTech Systems, Inc.   RE: 5/15/9X <u>City Times</u>
1444 Soneigh Way   ad for Word Processors
Damon, PA 09876

Dear Ms. Sweet:

While it may seem odd for a Philosophy professor to be responding to
your ad for Word Processors, today's economy has rendered many of
yesterday's tenets entirely revocable.

I am highly skilled in WordPerfect for Windows, as your ad requested.
Six years of intense analysis and serious writing account for my
<u>indisputable command</u> of this invaluable computer program.

In addition, I offer your firm the <u>maturity to deal effectively</u> with
clients, executives, and co-workers, particularly those under pressure.
My <u>written and verbal communication skills</u> are advanced, which may
prove extremely useful to your staff in the preparation of customer
materials, reports, and presentations.

Let me assure you that I do not consider this position a stop-gap by any
means. After working in academia for nearly 17 years, the opportunity
to join a fast paced leader in the business world is a stimulating one.

I hope you will contact me so that we might meet.

Sincerely,

Christopher J. Rinaldi
(555) 456-7890 home

Mr. Oliver Orrington
Orrington Engineering
52 Eberhart Avenue
Traverse City, MI 09876

RE: 1/2/9X <u>City Times</u>
    ad: Word Processing
    Format Specialist

Dear Mr. Orrington:

I am an accomplished Word Processing Format Specialist with considerable experience in desktop publishing. With my skills, your office can dramatically increase its productivity and output -- even meeting impossibly tight deadlines for your clients!

Opening promises a benefit.

<u>I am fluent in the following:</u>
WordPerfect
WordPerfect for Windows
Excel
Lotus 1-2-3
AmiPro

<u>I can operate in both MAC and IBM environments.</u>

<u>I am a true artist at bringing information to life
with dazzling charts, graphs, and illustrations.</u>

And, I am available to begin working for you immediately. Part-time or full-time, I will be a dedicated employee. Please give me a call at (555) 456-7890 and we can start producing eye-popping reports and presentations.

Thank you.

Rudolf P. Osborn

G. R. Rodriguez
Vice President   RE: Your ad for a
P.O. Box 1111   System Technician
<u>City Times</u>   <u>City Times</u>, 1/13/9X
Brewster, NH 09876

To Vice President Rodriguez:

As a systems technician for PageNet, one of the country's leading paging services companies, I have earned superior performance reviews for each of the last 3 years.

Now I would like to bring this reputation to a growing firm, such as yours, that can benefit from my knowledge and experience.

In return for the opportunity to expand my territory and compensation, I offer expertise in installing and maintaining transmitters and paging terminal equipment developed through 3 years of solid field experience, the ability to adhere to a full service schedule without supervision as well as a positive, pleasant manner in my dealings with both personal and business customers. Naturally, I hold FCC certification and a valid driver's license.

Hiring someone with my experience will certainly save your company the cost of training a less experienced technician. If you will page me at (555) 456-7890 and leave your number, I will call at once to set up an appointment.

Sincerely,

Bethany I. Allen

Resumé enclosed

Mr. Miguel Buitta
Senior Executive Vice President
TechnoSphere Technologies
1800 Coronet Circle
Reston, VA 09876

Dear Mr. Buitta:

Given the advanced technology with which you and I deal on a daily basis, I rarely have a business conversation these days that doesn't require translation. Speaking with you on the phone earlier today was a pleasure!

As promised, I have enclosed my resumé, which details my 17-year tenure with ICM. To preview the information on my resumé, I will call your attention to an achievement of particular interest to TechnoSphere -- one that also doubles as the highlight of my career:

> Emerging technologies such as (GPS) Global Positioning System and character recognition techniques were the focus of my study in an effort to reduce the skyrocketing cost of data conversion.

> Not only did my efforts <u>lower conversion costs</u> across the board, but this technology became <u>vital to U.S. efforts in the Gulf War</u>. GPS satellite signals allowed our troops to navigate accurately around the featureless desert environment.

My knowledge of, and experience with, an extensive array of computer technology and highly sophisticated applications enable me to conceive and spearhead a comprehensive range of innovative projects for TechnoSphere. Such projects will undoubtedly produce results that have far-reaching implications within the industry, science and health, the U.S. business community, and the international scene.

It would be a genuine opportunity to apply my unusual capabilities to help TechnoSphere seize significant, not to mention lucrative, contracts that will add to the organization's overall reputation and presence.

Thank you for your interest and willingness to meet with me. I will call shortly to schedule an appointment.

Sincerely,

Raj Jaarynharoon
(555) 456-7890

Mr. Bart Holmes
Human Resource Director   RE: MIS Manager position
555-456-7890 fax   advertised 4/5/9X <u>City Times</u>

Dear Mr. Holmes:

As an experienced and successful MIS Manager, I offer you <u>all</u> of the qualifications listed in your advertisement -- and then some. I am, therefore, faxing you my resumé with this letter.

As my resumé illustrates, I possess the track record, technical knowledge, and expertise to effectively:

- Design, develop, implement, and support all MIS functions.

- Evaluate, recommend, and purchase hardware, software, and supplies.

- Manage, develop, and support multiplatform environments.

- Demonstrate proficiency with Appletalk, Novell, and Windows.

My work at a leading architectural design firm expanded my abilities to apply the best that today's computer technology has to offer from a more creative point of view than many other MIS Managers may possess. As a result, I have an unusual talent for turning challenges into solutions that can yield profitable results.

The benefit of working for a smaller firm is that I had the opportunity to handle a range of responsibilities. The downside is that my salary history may not be in line with industry standards. I would be pleased to provide you with more information on this when we have the chance to meet. If you will contact me at (555) 765-4321, I will be pleased to set up an appointment.

Sincerely,

Michael Manning
(555) 765-4321

This unusually bold approach works because the candidate meets every one of the requirements listed in the ad.

Ms. Althea Wilcox
Director, Personnel   RE: Your ad for a
Broadham Technical Systems, Inc.   Network Administrator,
Elizabeth, NJ 09876   <u>City Times</u>, 11/20/9X

Dear Ms. Wilcox:

Your advertisement addresses my qualifications so ideally, one would think we'd met. And we should -- because I can offer you the **_precise_** skills for which you're searching.

<u>You seek the ability to:</u>	<u>Do I possess?</u>
Train and support local and remote area network users.	YES
Plan and support Windows NT-based local area network.	YES
Manage security, capacity planning, database support for SQL Server database and maintain LAN/nationwide office links.	YES
Deal effectively with Windows and provide SQL Server database support.	YES and YES

I hope you'll agree that your needs and my capabilities are a perfect match because it would be a thrill to join a firm with the technological talent yours employs.

In fact, I am not currently in the job market, but am responding <u>only to your ad</u>. Therefore, I would appreciate maintaining confidentiality. Please contact me at home at (555) 456-7890 evenings or weekends, or by mail at the address printed above. I'd be pleased to set up a meeting whenever it's convenient for you.

> *Attention grabber.*

Sincerely,

Lionel N. Ruminjan

Mr. George Misal
Vice President
Digital Equipment Corporation
1234 Main Street
Encino, CA 09876

Dear Mr. Misal:

My immediate superior describes me as "a unique combination of left brain logic and right brain creativity." My engineering background drives my methodical approach to solving problems. My creativity produces the flexibility to assess and assemble numerous alternatives.

Clever opening!

I am responding to your ad for a Communications Specialist because my left brain logic has determined that my skills are ideally suited to fulfill the responsibilities of this position.

My exceptional communication skills allow me to either distill complex technical information into customer requirements, or define customer requirements and then apply the appropriate technology. As a result, your firm will set a new standard in customer satisfaction. My experience with multiple vehicles for conveying information -- such as video tape, multimedia presentations, radio spots, and national TV programs -- will enable you to serve a broader client base more cost-effectively.

I am a quick study and have educated myself on subjects from business financial models to Nuclear Magnetic Resonance Spectroscopy (NMR). Currently, I am responsible for aftermarket Personal Computer Multimedia products in both the commercial and retail markets.

My right brain creativity would welcome the opportunity to meet in person and explore the opportunities my unique strengths will bring to Digital.

I will call you shortly to schedule an appointment.

Sincerely,

Rick Abrams
555-456-7890 weekdays
555-765-5432 evenings

AdvantaCom, Inc.
2108 State Line   RE: Software/Hardware
Kansas City, MO 09876   Senior Executive

Dear Search Committee:

It's not like riding a bicycle! Contributing to the planning, promoting, and day-to-day operations of an emerging technologies company like AdvantaCom is <u>not the same</u> as running a company in the fashion, financial, or fishing industries.

After 7 years directing the operations of an East Coast competitor and more than 8 years managing software engineering … I should know! Unlike any other industry, ours demands of its Senior Executives a level of technical sophistication that can only be the product of hands-on, in-depth, unfailing relevant experience … *precisely what I offer AdvantaCom!*

I am <u>exceptionally articulate</u> in a diverse range of hardware and software, client/server technology, systems programming, and database management. I also possess the <u>demonstrated ability</u> to successfully apply the strategies and principles fundamental to building and growing a business in today's volatile economy.

This background arms me to lead AdvantaCom in generating results as impressive as those I helped my current organization achieve:

    -Margins surpassing industry averages by 23%.

    -Operations productivity 45% over previous levels.

    -Domestic market share growth exceeding 30%.

    -Hardware products introduced to previously untapped (by us) global marketplaces, delivering $12 million in sales in first year alone along with a 97% customer satisfaction rating.

My expertise in technology and management are at your disposal, as is my proven track record. It would be an honor to join an organization with your reputation and promise. You may reach me at (555) 456-7890 during business hours and at (555) 765-4321 at home.

Sincerely,

Hugh J. McNeil

Without providing more detail than is necessary, this jobhunter arms the recruiter with valuable information: his field, his specialty, and what he offers an employer.

Ms. Sylvia McCormack
President
McCormack Recruiting Co.
5 Liberty Circle
Sacramento, CA 09876

Dear Ms. McCormack:

In today's difficult economy, you undoubtedly receive hundreds of resumés from people seeking employment. However, you have built a career on the ability to recognize marketable talents, which I possess -- in-depth experience, focused expertise, flexibility, adaptability, commitment, and a highly effective management style.

Excellent opening for recruiter letter

My current employer's economic health makes it advisable for me to seek a new situation as soon as possible. I am therefore taking the liberty of forwarding my resumé for your review.

My specific niche is the design and implementation of new technology for electrical subsystems, but I can contribute effectively within a variety of engineering environments.

My background, professional experience, and work style equip me to offer a rare overview of the field along with a profound grasp of project details. This mix is unusual among professionals in my field, and it is essential to the employer actively seeking innovative solutions in emerging technologies.

I look to your expertise for assistance in my search and will call you early next week to see whether we can schedule a meeting. I thank you in advance for your consideration.

Sincerely,

Todd Wychowsky
(555) 455-7890 home
(555) 765-4321 work

In this letter and the three that follow, the writers successfully adopted the perfect no-nonsense approach for use with busy theatrical agents who receive hundreds, possibly thousands, of head shots in response to a single ad.

Ms. Ann Houseman
The Actor's Resource
3467 Seventh Avenue
New York, NY 09876

Dear Ms. Houseman:

Please consider me for extra work. I work like a dog and I'm docile as a lamb. Thank you.

Sincerely,

Nancy Neuhart
(555) 456-7890 Service

P.S.: This is the first time I have sent you my picture and resumé.

Enclosures

Ms. Ann Houseman
The Actor's Resource
3467 Seventh Avenue
New York, NY 09876

RE: Your June 5, 199X *Backstage* ad
for "The Innocents of Youth"

Dear Ms. Houseman:

Naiveté, charm, wide-eyed purity, and a belief that everything will turn
out for the best. Such innocence still exists. It's portrayed in my head
shots, which are enclosed.

And, golly, it's exactly what you're looking for.

Best,

Anthony Kilpatrick
(555) 456-7890 telephone service

Ms. Ann Houseman
The Actor's Resource
3467 Seventh Avenue
New York, NY 09876

Dear Ms. Houseman:

In high school, I was voted "Most Likely to Blend into a Crowd," making me ideal for extra work. Thank you for considering me.

Sincerely,

John E. Jennings
Service: (555) 456-7890

Enclosures: Resumé and head shots

Ms. Ann Houseman
The Actor's Resource   RE: Your 12/01/9X
3467 Seventh Avenue   *Backstage* ad for
New York, NY 09876   "New Faces"

Dear Ms. Houseman:

I have enclosed my resumé and head shots, as requested in your
advertisement. Yes, I have done stand-up comedy and I have a good
corporate look. Please keep me in mind.

Sincerely,

Rock Vermillion
Telephone service: (555) 456-7890

Ms. Althea Adams
Anytime, Anywhere Productions
1234 Bleeker Street
New York, NY 09876

Dear Ms. Adams:

With the plethora of producers currently looking for employment, you are certainly hiring in a buyer's market.

Before sifting through hundreds of resumés, however, I urge you to spend a moment that may save you hours of needless interviewing. Who will add the proper mix of creativity, professionalism, and award-winning talent to your staff? The answer may be in your hands right now.

As a writer and producer, I have created feature films as well as historical epics, children's educational programs, and contemporary television serials -- as listed on the enclosed resumé -- both here and abroad. The broad scope of projects with which I have been involved demonstrates **my range and ability to function in any milieu.** The fact that several of my pieces were awarded presitigious honors illustrates **the quality of my work.**

> <u>Rest assured, however, that each of these films was completed at or under budget and on time.</u>

A personal discussion will convince you that there is no need to spend hours interviewing other candidates. I will call you shortly.

Sincerely,

Alan Hoopes
(555) 765-4321 Telephone

To see the results this heartfelt letter produced, see the follow-up in Letter 5-15.

Ms. Leonore Valerio
Lincoln Center Institute
New York, NY 09876

RE: Your ad for a
Teaching Artist,
<u>Community Times</u>, 4/10/9X

Dear Ms. Valerio:

What a delight it is to discover a school that recognizes the value of promoting dance among its students and actually allocates funding for this vital intention!

In applying for the teaching position at LCI, I offer you a rare mix of talents and experience, as described in detail on the enclosed resumé. My **comprehensive training** in the United States and abroad is complemented by my experience as a **member in such diverse companies** as the Belgrade National Theatre, the Ballet Hispanico of New York, and the Julliard Dance Ensemble. Both have equipped me to introduce a far broader range of methods, techniques, styles, music, and interpretation than many others in the field.

Throughout more than 20 years in dance and dance education, I have experienced my own joy as well as that of students of both sexes and every age as they acquire much needed self-confidence by expressing themselves through movement. The opportunity to continue such a worthwhile endeavor at the Lincoln Center Institute would be as thrilling as it would be rewarding.

I will contact you within the next several days to further explore this exciting possibility.

Thank you for your consideration.

Sincerely,

Isadora Ilianya
(555) 456-7890

Director
Radio, TV and Film Department
State University
P.O. Box 1111
University City, MD 09876

To the Department Director:

In your search for someone to coordinate your Student Film Projects, I present you with the ideal candidate: myself. My resumé, which is enclosed, details my 7 years of experience handling precisely the responsibilities this position entails.

I am adept at managing the complexities of scheduling time, staff resources, and equipment -- relieving you of these burdensome tasks. I invariably maintain the utmost diplomacy when dealing with each of hundreds of young, creative students on a deadline -- saving you needless turmoil.

If you will contact me at (555) 456-7890 day or night, I will be pleased to visit your campus whenever your schedule permits.

I look forward to meeting you.

Sincerely,

William A. Galvan

Dr. Lawrence Ahearn
Milford School System
18 Central Avenue
Milford, NY 09876

Dear Dr. Ahearn:

As a father with three children in the Milford school system, I hope that each of my children receives not only a sound education, but that she acquires a perspective of life outside the school walls. With my business background and teaching credentials, I am equipped to offer both to the Milford students.

After 20 years in corporate business training, I am now shifting my focus to educating within the school system. This year, I completed my education credits, fulfilled my student teaching requirements at Milford Middle School, and passed my certification examinations. Having just received word from Albany that my Certificate of Qualifications has been issued, I thought this would be the ideal time to write to you.

Dr. Ahearn, my diverse background offers Milford students a unique opportunity to discover how their studies have practical application in what they call "the real world."

I would welcome the chance to discuss any openings that may arise under your aegis. I will contact you soon to see whether we might meet. Or you may reach me at (555) 765-4321.

Most sincerely,

Andrew L. Moses

Here is a novel approach that works for a graduating student with no relevant background.

Ms. Regina Connors
Santa Fe Regional Educational Program
54 Desert View Drive
Santa Fe, NM 12345

Dear Ms. Connors:

With great excitement, I am responding to your ad for a Kindergarten Teacher. The opportunity to teach in the school system that fostered my interest in education is a thrilling one.

Because I have recently switched from the business world to teaching, my resumé may not provide the information you require (it is enclosed, nonetheless). Instead, allow me to excerpt from a recommendation provided by my advisor, Lynn Karyli:

> "Lauren never seems to choose the easy way; she takes the most demanding courses, opts to work in the most challenging teaching situations, attempts the most innovative and difficult teaching approaches and volunteers time and energy to extracurricular activities. And, in all her endeavors, she is successful …

> "… It should be noted, that in the short period of a year and half, Lauren won the praise and admiration of her professors and her peers. She was selected as research assistant for a project on children's response to the arts. She is a highly respected member of her peer group, valued both for her leadership capabilities and for her constructive feedback and support of the efforts of others …

> "… Thus, Lauren is a model for all who are associated with her and to all she brings enthusiasm and energy, sensitivity, thoughtfulness, and thoroughness and above all, a love of children and of life."

This recommendation (in its entirety) is also enclosed. I am anxious to pursue this opportunity and to meet you in person. I will take the liberty of calling you to schedule an appointment.

Sincerely,

Lauren Quay
(555) 765-4321

Ms. Lucille Lockhart
Vice President, Human Resources
CompuTech Industries
47 Pratt Street
Hartford, CT 09876

RE: Your ad in the <u>Hartford Courant</u>, Sunday, May 8, 199X
    for an Assistant to the President

Dear Ms. Lockhart:

Impeccable interpersonal skills. Organizational and supervisory abilities. Attention to detail. Your ad describes my strengths precisely!

<u>People Power</u>: As a teacher in the public school system for three years, I am adept at dealing with people -- from "by the book" career administrators to the high school bully, from irate parents to the shy underachiever, from goal-oriented department heads to aggressive textbook sales representatives.

<u>Management Skills</u>: As a homemaker raising two children, I mastered the ability to spearhead three projects simultaneously while supervising two distinct groups of youngsters, maintaining my patience and my good temper all the while.

<u>Accuracy</u>: As a volunteer for a local hospital, I coordinated the ever-changing schedules of 50 unpaid workers for 5 years with nary a "foul-up."

Handling these responsibilities provided me with a <u>different kind of experience</u>: the kind the corporate world just doesn't offer -- and the kind that proves invaluable once you enter this world, as I'd like to do now.

I hope you'll consider me a serious candidate for the position of Assistant to the President. I certainly would take the job very seriously, proving an asset to the President and to the company.

Sincerely,

Frances Dougherty
Home Phone: (555) 765-4321

Superintendent of Schools
The Provincetown School Committee
High School Annex
Charles Street
Provincetown, MA 09876

Dear Sir or Madam:

I am a teacher of English at the Forsyth Satellite Academy in New York City. In May, I will complete the Master's Program in English Education at New York University, where I have the honor of having been selected as the Graduate Valedictory Speaker. This summer, I will receive 6 postgraduate credits as a participant in the New York City Writing Project at The City University of New York. Before entering the field of Education, I enjoyed 8 years in accounting -- a field I left voluntarily in January 199X to pursue a long felt desire to teach, motivate, and guide students in their use of the language and appreciation of literature. I am thrilled with my decision to switch careers!

With these unique strengths, I write because I am moving to Cape Cod in August and I seek a position as a teacher of English in the Provincetown School District.

I recognize that there may be a shortage of openings. While my primary goal is to secure a full-time position teaching English, I would like to offer my services in any capacity for which you might find my background suitable. I will gladly work on a part-time basis or as a substitute. I enclose a resumé of my business and educational experience along with my most recent evaluation, made by my practicum supervisor.

I would welcome the privilege of meeting with you to discuss any appropriate position that you may have in your district. I can come to see you on very short notice should you be willing to meet with me; you can reach me at (555) 234-3456. Thank you for your interest.

Warm regards,

George Andrew Hillman

The lack of a resumé is not holding this homemaker and mother from applying for a job. Her letter sounds and looks as professional as that of any executive.

Ms. Chris Harper
New York Foundling Hospital
Two Sixth Avenue   RE: Child Care Worker
New York, NY 09876   Seton Day Care Center

Dear Ms. Harper:

Seton Day Care, its children, and their parents deserve the very best Child Care Worker you can find. May I offer myself as a candidate who can meet this tough standard?

<u>My experience working with children is as extensive as it is diverse.</u> As a mother of two, I have performed the multiple and continual duties that every newborn requires. As a volunteer in both the nursery school and first grade classroom environments, I have dealt effectively with children at an age when your every breath and action contributes to the shaping of their personalities, demeanor, and morals. I have also cared for older children in my home, both for pay and as a courtesy to other mothers, so I am well aware of the challenges and rewards of this vital responsibility.

<u>Supporting my practical experience is a thorough educational background and hands-on work in the field.</u> In earning my degree in Family and Consumer Studies, my relevant studies included courses in Child Psychology, Child Development, Sociology of the Family, and Family Relationships. In addition, I completed field work in a day-care facility in the Bronx.

<u>Personally, I offer you the following strengths</u>: I possess a calm attitude and superb understanding of children's needs. Many people are surprised by how comfortable their children feel with me. As a mother, I empathize with other parents and find it easy to build a productive rapport.

Although I am in the process of updating my resumé, I am extremely interested in pursuing this opportunity and I did not want to delay contacting you. At your convenience, I would like to meet with you to explore the opportunity of working together. If you will contact me at (555) 456-7890 (day or evening), we can schedule a meeting, at which I will present you with my completed resumé.

Thank you in advance for your consideration

Sincerely,

Felicity Adnagi
(555) 456-7890

Dr. Lucille Klingman
8 Hawthorne Avenue
Milltown, WY 09876

Dear Dr. Klingman:

After 12 years as a Dental Hygienist, I know all there is to know about routine oral hygiene, orthodontic hygiene, and pediatric hygiene.

> However, my experience extends further than this … and further than most other hygienists.

I have performed in a frenetically busy multi-practitioner environment and a teaching facility, as well. As a result, I am expertly capable of managing the demands of overworked dentists, nervous adults, and hyperactive children. I can instantly develop a comforting rapport with patients of any age.

Now, I would like to apply my expertise to the needs of a small, local practice. From the sound of your advertisement in the City Times this past Sunday, my skills would be a perfect match for your setting.

If you will contact me at my home number, I will be in touch to set up a meeting at your convenience. I would greatly appreciate your professional courtesy in refraining from contacting my present employer.

Sincerely,

Howard MacKenzie
Home telephone: (555) 456-7890

If you were hiring, it's likely you'd find it tough to turn down an interview with someone so skilled and dedicated. Despite being out of the workforce for years, this jobhunter knows how to get results!

Mr. Albert Girannelli
P.O. Box 1111
City Times
Clayton, MO 09876

Dear Mr. Girannelli:

Your ad for a Social Worker caught my attention since I would like to rejoin the profession after several years as a homemaker and mother. With my education, experience, and commitment to human services, I possess all the qualifications you seek.

I have a BS in Learning Disabilities, MSW degree, and state licensure. For 5 years, I worked at a facility providing subacute care and rehabilitation services to children and their families with a variety of special health needs, receiving regular praise from my superiors for my clinical and interpersonal skills. More recently, I performed over 10,000 hours of volunteer work with substance abusers while raising three children.

Through my efforts over the years, I have remained abreast of new issues and ideas in human services. I would be surprised if you were able to find a more dedicated employee than I will be, or one more ready to contribute once again by performing first-class assessments, treatments, consultation, and training.

Enclosed you will find my resumé, a copy of my state license, and references. If there is anything else I can provide, please let me know. I am anxious to meet with you as soon as possible.

Sincerely,

Suzanne Collins
(555) 765-4321

Ms. Miranda S. Lewin
Director of Staff
The Trent-Bridges Academy
1233 Academy Road
Stamford, CT 09876

Dear Ms. Lewin:

If your Speech Pathology Department has room for a skilled, enthusiastic, and committed Speech Therapist, I hope you will consider me.

This June, I will receive my BS from State University's School of Speech. I have already begun supplementing my formal training in Speech and Language Pathology with several practicums and internships, all of which inspire me to continue contributing to this valuable profession while preparing for my Masters and Certification.

Through my work with stroke patients, stutterers, and those with cleft palate and articulation disorders, I have acquired hands-on experience that may enhance the success and reputation your department already enjoys. My grades and evaluations have been consistently superior, validating my skill as well as my ability to work harmoniously with co-workers.

Of greatest value to you, however, is my commitment to each and every patient with whom I work. My objective is to improve their lives by improving their ability to communicate and their self-esteem.

If these are the qualities you seek, I hope you will contact me. I will be happy to visit your office for an interview, at your convenience.

Sincerely,

Luna Moss
555-456-7890 Telephone

Dr. Phoebe Williamson
The Sacred Heart Academy
40 Lakeview Drive   RE: Your <u>City Times</u> ad
Galveston, TX 09876   for a Registered Nurse

Dear Dr. Williamson:

Given the reputation for excellence that you maintain at The Sacred Heart Academy, you hold equally rigorous standards in your search for a Registered Nurse to care for your students and faculty.

Excellence is exactly what I can deliver, along with an unusually strong background in health care.

My resumé, which is enclosed, details the depth of my experience with newborns, grade-level children, adolescents, and young adults of college age. As you'll see, I have worked as a Student Health Nurse, Camp Nurse, Family Camp Coordinator, hospital Staff Nurse in labor and delivery, and Nursing Care Coordinator. These assignments, along with my work as a Nurse Coordinator for a Perinatal HIV Transmission Study, honed my ability to deal with children and their parents with understanding, warmth, and humor.

During the past several years, I reduced my workload outside the home while raising two sons. I am now ready and eager to return to Nursing, and to continue combining exceptional medical care with compassionate patient care.

The opportunity to pursue these objectives as a member of Sacred Heart's highly respected staff is an important one. I do hope that you'll allow me to present my qualifications to you in person.

I look forward to hearing from you.

Sincerely,

Kerry A. Childs
(555) 765-4321

Human Resources Director
St. Andrew's Memorial Hospital
4500 Main Street
West Lafayette, GA 09876

To the Director of Human Resources
for St. Andrew's Hospital:

I am responding to your advertisement for a Registered Nurse to direct your Quality Improvement Program because I can supply *precisely* the background you require.

<u>My resumé supports the following introduction</u>:

-I earned my MS in nursing at State College.

-I have worked for 3 years as Assistant Director of Quality Assurance under Janice Powers at State Hospital.

-I am adept at interpreting quality assurance standards to ensure adherence to DPH and JCAHO guidelines.

-I have assisted in the creation of quality improvement policies, compiling statistical data and writing narrative reports that summarize quality assurance findings.

-I have directed a variety of health center personnel and worked with numerous patients in order to evaluate the effectiveness of this quality improvement program.

Of greatest importance is my commitment to ensuring comprehensive, easily accessible, high-quality care. My in-depth experience has prepared me to define and implement quality improvement standards that function in full compliance with existing health center policies and procedures.

I am fully prepared to assume complete responsibility for directing a Quality Improvement Program, and I would welcome the opportunity to explore how my skills meet your specific needs.

Sincerely,

Brenda Miller
(555) 456-7890

This jobhunter has categorized his abilities so that the letter can be easily skimmed—or read in full with greater meaning. Either way, any reader will be convinced that he is a qualified candidate worth interviewing.

Ms. Lillian Bytters
SVC Pharmacy
8700 American Way   RE: Your 2/25/9X ad for a
Industry City, NJ 09876   Senior Pharmacist

Dear Ms. Bytters:

My qualifications are ideal for the position you've advertised -- and, as my current employer has been acquired by a major retailer, I am available to you almost immediately. My resumé, which is enclosed, details my training, licensure, and professional experience. Allow me to highlight my strengths and capabilities for you here:

Competency, Experience: I routinely and accurately ensure proper filling and dispensing of prescriptions; evaluate physician drug orders and patient profiles for appropriateness of therapy, dose, and dosing regimens; clarify and correct problematic drug orders.

Interaction with Physicians and Patients: I effectively obtain patient medical and medication histories; answer inquiries from physicians and patients regarding drug therapies, drug dosing and administration, drug interactions, adverse effects, and new products; provide direct patient counseling and education; advise patients on prescription-related insurance benefits; monitor patient profiles for drug interactions and allergies; provide courteous customer service and professional relations.

Accurate Recordkeeping: I ensure proper documentation of pharmacy records in accordance with state law, prescription inventory control and management within budgetary guidelines.

Insurance and Claims Expertise: I operate automatic claims verification programs and ensure proper billing to third-party insurance providers; correspond with insurance providers regarding patient eligibility and benefits; maintain account receivables records for third-party payers.

Inventory Control: I correspond with wholesalers to determine the availability and cost of drug products; track costs of goods sold, sales, gross margin percent, accounts payable, and inventory turns on a weekly basis; maintain records of prescription sales and volume, and compare these to previous periods in order to improve inventory management.

If you can set aside some time next week, I would be pleased to visit your headquarters. I will call you within the next few days to schedule a convenient time to meet.

With best regards,

John G. Miller
Work telephone: 555-456-7890
Home telephone: 555-765-4321

P.O. Box 100
Los Angeles County
40040 San Cerrino Boulevard
Los Angeles, CA 09876

To Los Angeles County Officials:

I am eager to present myself as a candidate for the Assistant Director of Emergency Medical Services for Los Angeles County. It has long been a dream of mine to contribute to the safety of residents and public protection professionals at the county level.

I am proud to report that, in addition to meeting all of the qualifications listed in your advertisement -- and being fully bilingual in Spanish and English -- I also offer you the following important strengths:

Diverse Supplemental Training: I have complemented my education and training, successfully completing additional courses in critical incident stress response, aircraft emergency incident management, emergency response to hazardous materials incidents, prehospital response to radiation accidents, emergency vehicle operation, poison control, and crash victim extrication.

Proven Ability to Perform: During my 12-year career with the Oakland Township Emergency Medical Service, I served as EVOC Instructor before being promoted from Paramedic to Lieutenant of Special Operations to Captain of the Training Division. Currently, I serve as the EMS Liaison to the Township's Medical Advisory Committee.

Solid Teaching Background: At Oakland Memorial Hospital's Institute of Emergency Medicine, I served as an Instructor for the Paramedic Training Program, EMT, and CPR training. I also directed the Oakland Police Department's Vehicle Extrication program.

Recognized for Excellence: Throughout my career, I have been noted for my contributions; I have received more than 50 Letters of Commendation, 19X1 and 19X2 Township Life Saving Medals, and the Fire Department's Award of Merit, among other distinctions.

Since your position offers an opportunity, location, and benefits package that are very appealing to me, my salary requirements are flexible. I would be honored if you would consider me a serious candidate.

Sincerely,

Juan Miranda
(555) 765-4321 work
(555) 456-7890 home

Mr. Angelo Adevon
Metro Health Club
4298 Eighth Avenue
Omaha, NE 09876

**Re: 8/19/9X ad for a
Personal Trainer**

Dear Mr. Adevon:

In our industry, turnover is high among training staff, and this often adversely affects customers' perceptions of a health club or fitness center. I can help your organization avoid this problem.

I have been in my current position for 9 years, and am only seeking alternate employment because our owner has decided to retire and close the facility. Not only do I have the experience to bring to your club, I also built a loyal base of "one-on-ones," many of whom are likely to follow me within reasonable geographic limits.

I am well-versed in a complete range of equipment, such as Aerobic (Stairmaster, treadmills, running machines, cross-country skiing, bicycles, Lifecycle and VersaClimber), Free weights, Universal, Eagle, and Nautilus. I have designed personal fitness programs for clients from ages 18 to 80, even working successfully with individuals required by their doctors to lose 100 pounds or more. My skill, rapport, and results have led many of my existing clients to introduce me to their friends, whom I have taken on as new clients.

If you're looking to add long lasting muscle to your training program, please contact me at (555) 456-7890 and we can schedule a time to get together.

Sincerely,

Bill Zeman

Ms. Aprile Longo
The Milanese Beauty Spa
50 Central Avenue
Greenwich, CT 09876

RE: <u>City Times</u> 5/20/9X ad for an Esthetician

Dear Ms. Longo:

When working with clients, my goals are to pamper the mind and body … soothe muscle tension … relieve stress … eliminate fatigue due to overwork …

… the very same benefits you'll enjoy when you add a professional, experienced esthetician to your staff. And few are as accomplished as I am.

Naturally, I am skilled at blending concentrated therapeutic oils for aromatherapy massage to create the optimal ambience for effective beauty treatments. But I am also well versed in a complete range of additional revitalizing regimes including facial and body skin care, body scrub and polishing, tissue toning, hydrotherapy, seaweed body mask, and detoxification.

> <u>The result is that by hiring me, you acquire a range of additional services to offer your clients for the price of a single, expert esthetician. Plus, I can bring with me an established, affluent base of regular clientele.</u>

I firmly believe in the importance of massage and esthetic treatments to combat stress and prevent illness, and would appreciate the opportunity to demonstrate my abilities first-hand.

If you would be kind enough to contact me at my home number, I will be pleased to schedule an appointment to discuss how my varied skills can relieve the pressure for you and your staff.

Cordially,

Susan Ellis Long
(555) 456-7890 home

Mr. Ellis Harnauer
Bay City Community Airport
1000 Aeroway
Bay City, IA 09876

Dear Mr. Harnauer:

Thank you for discussing with me the opening for a Noise Abatement Officer at County Airport. Putting my training to work in this environment is an exciting opportunity that I am anxious to discuss with you further.

When we meet, I will be pleased to relate the strengths I can bring to your department. Briefly, these include:

-A focused, comprehensive educational background culminating with my graduating with honors from State Aeronautical University

-Additional elective study in airport development and operations, technical report writing, government and aviation, avionics for aviators, aviation law

-Unparalleled ability to organize, schedule, implement, and follow up on assignments, developed through 4 years of successful self-employment

-Commitment, dedication, and loyalty grounded in a strong desire to capitalize on my training and return to aviation

In addition, I possess a valid commercial pilot license and I am well-versed in the use of computer technology for input of aircraft operational data, running database management programs, and preparing reports for presentation. I am equipped to perform routine maintenance of noise monitoring equipment including calibration at remote monitoring sites and testing of central system components.

My resumé, which is enclosed, provides complete details. I am looking forward to seeing you on Wednesday, November 19 at 9:00 a.m.

Sincerely,

Serge Fabien
(555) 456-7890

Mr. Peter K. Lowenstein
Package Express, Inc.
67-578 North Airport Way
Industry City, NJ 09876

Dear Mr. Lowenstein:

I am responding to your ad for a Casual Van Driver. My background
and abilities provide you with exactly the experience your ad requests.

I possess a valid commercial driver's license class B with hazardous
material and airbrakes endorsements. My driving record is solid. Having
lived all my life in and around Industry City, I am thoroughly familiar
with the entire metro area.

As a consumer, I am repeatedly faced with discourteous service in many
areas of my daily life. As a result, I make it a point to deliver a high
level of service whenever I am called upon to deal with customers --
and I would do the same for you, making me an exemplary
representative of Package Express.

Although I am looking for a full-time position, I would willingly accept
the challenge described in your ad: that successful performance could
lead to regular part-time or full-time employment.

Thank you for your consideration.

Sincerely,

Janice Robertson
(555) 765-4321

Mr. Victor Britman
The Golden Palate
2100 Douglass Street
Victoria, British Columbia
Canada TAL OCO

RE: Your Ad for a Wine Specialist, October 5 City Times.

Dear Mr. Britman:

Appropriate training? Check.
(See enclosed resumé.)

Minimum 5 years of experience? Check.
(I have 11.)

Knowledgeable in international and domestic wines? Check.
(Can one truly be a Wine Specialist without appreciating
the excitement of a pungent Cloudy Bay *sauvignon blanc* or
the promise *meritage* brings to California?)

Willing to relocate? Check.
(My bag is packed, my passport valid.)

The only thing left is for us to meet.
I will call you in the morning on Wednesday, the 14th
to schedule an appointment.

As you can see, my enthusiasm has been uncorked!

Until we meet,

Jean-Claude Mertrand
(555) 456-7890

Box YR87
<u>City Times</u>
New York, NY 09876

Re: 10/9/9X ad for a Chauffeur

To the Holder of Box YR87:

STOP! Don't read another resumé -- except mine. My 5 years' experience as a Chauffeur for the CEO of a Fortune 500 company equips me with the precise qualifications you seek.

MERGE my professional appearance and demeanor with the ability to perform around the clock, discretion, and the utmost caution -- and you secure the most reliable, personable chauffeur available.

TURN your attention to the telephone and call me at (555) 765-4321, and I will come in at once for an interview. My current employer has retired to the Caribbean so I am available to begin working immediately.

I thank you in advance for your consideration.

Sincerely,

J. Darrell Freeman

Here's a jobhunter who knows her industry! The opening, body, and close are consistent with her knowledge and tone of voice.

Ms. Monica Frick
The Frick Publishing Company   RE: Your ad for an
1871 Memphis Avenue   Editorial Assistant
Nashville, TN 09876   <u>City Times</u>, 11/20/9X

Dear Ms. Frick:

The value of your delightful AspenGlow mysteries, which I avidly consumed as a child, remains unmatched in my life.

From this series I acquired the ability to persevere in the search for a more effective method ... skepticism when faced with a too obvious solution ... the curiosity to discover what more a person can offer. Each of these traits was inspired by AspenGlow. All are qualifications the successful editor must possess.

The older I get, the more I appreciate what Frick Publishing and AspenGlow brought to my life. And as I am still far from retirement, I am able to bring these talents back to you. I have enclosed my resumé to demonstrate that my experience is as relevant as my enthusiasm.

So that you may consider me as a serious candidate for the position of Editorial Assistant, I will call you shortly to see if we might meet.

Eager to meet you, I am sincerely,

Karen Innis-Gales
(555) 456-7890 Telephone

Mr. Winston Stanhope
American Products Corporation
1234 Main Street   RE: <u>City Times</u> ad 3/16/9X for an
Pittsburgh, PA 09876   Employee Benefits Manager

Dear Mr. Stanhope:

Employee Benefits are as vital to your organization as they are to your staff. However, the details inherent in most benefits plans can make administering them cumbersome and time-consuming -- which is why you now seek an experienced professional. In me, you have found one.

As you'll see on the enclosed resumé, I have managed all aspects of a comprehensive benefits program, including complex health care programs and COBRA. Of special value to you, given your pending acquisition of U.S. Consumer Goods, is my expertise in managing all types of qualified retirement plans and nonqualified executive programs, <u>meeting the combined needs of both the company and the employee</u>.

In uniting U.S. Consumer Goods' plan with yours, my unique experience is essential to <u>ensuring proper fiduciary compliance and accurate tax reporting</u> in a regulatory environment as volatile as ours is today. I am adept at plan design, administration, and recordkeeping. I have worked closely with providers to enhance investment management and <u>significantly improve cash flow and fund returns</u>.

I'd like to discuss this and other ways in which I can bring you genuine effectiveness in your Employee Benefits program, and genuine cost-effectiveness to your bottom line.

Sincerely,

Drew Johns
(555) 456-7890 work
(555) 765-4321 home

Ms. April Mendorff
Mendorff Personnel Agency
18800 Olive Street Road
St. Louis, MO 09876

Dear Ms. Mendorff:

Thank you for your time and the information you gave me during our phone conversation this morning. I have enclosed my resumé, as you requested, and appreciate any leads you can provide.

Permit me to summarize what is on my resumé. My training experience covers <u>corporate personnel</u> (for PrimeFirst Bancorporation) as well as automotive industry <u>sales professionals</u> (for General Motors).

<u>I have effectively</u>:

    -Conducted needs analyses.

    -Designed specialized training programs.

    -Designed classroom instruction curricula.

    -Taught one-on-one.

    -Created and administered a Management Development Program to support PrimeFirst's domestic operations.

I am outgoing and hard working. My natural enthusiasm supports my ability to teach, inspire, and motivate others from the entry level trainee to participants in Senior Management Training Programs.

Lets his personality shine through

I will contact you shortly to see when we might get together. I look forward to discovering whether I can assist your clients in achieving their training objectives.

Sincerely,

Howard MacNeil
(555) 456-7890

Mr. Robert L. Gorchin
Boston Transportation Authority
24 Manchester Place   RE: <u>Job Posting No. M75-4AB-96</u>
Boston, MA 09876   <u>Engineer, L&P Training</u>

Dear Mr. Gorchin:

While many candidates may possess the engineering background necessary to fill the opening in your training department, I am able to offer more. My unique mastery of diverse, advanced computer applications equips me to create and implement state-of-the-art training programs that reflect the latest technological developments.

For example:

- I am **fluent** in Basic, Hp Basic and COBOL languages; **experienced** working within DOS, Windows, Novell Netware environments; using WordPerfect, Pagemaker, Harvard Graphics, Paradox, Autocad, Photoshop, Flowchart, PowerPoint, multimedia, and other technologies to create interesting, informative programs for trainees **at every level of sophistication.**

- Demonstrating my ability to **operate effectively with outside agencies,** I worked closely with the Department of Defense, the Federal Aviation Administration and commercial vendors to create CBT programs that train end-users to become completely familiar with a product. Of particular relevance to BTA is my development of a simulator that **saved my employer more than $75K** in training costs.

- Through **17 years' engineering experience,** I have dealt successfully with test equipment, troubleshooting electronic circuitry, computers, and personnel training.

I am currently involved in developing troubleshooting aids, documenting test procedures, and systems specifications.

My experience with electronics, computers, program development, and training equips me to make a significant contribution to your training capabilities. I would be happy to meet with you at your convenience.

Sincerely,

Benjamin Ciryto
(555) 765-4321

Ms. Alexandra Samora
Human Resources Director
Americana Corporation
12 Richardson Plaza
Blue Grass, IA 09876

Regarding: March 23 <u>City Times</u> ad
for Director, Management
and Quality Training

Dear Ms. Samora:

<u>To move forward powerfully, effectively, and rapidly, today's
employees must align themselves with common goals and
with common ways to achieve these goals.</u>

Invariably, in promoting the concept of goal-oriented performance
management, the organizations with which I have worked were pleased
to discover that what's missing in many other quality initiatives is
precisely what **I** have learned in over 16 years of building high-
performance teams. I have *combined* my methodology with the tools of
quality and process management to create a synergy that is far superior
to either approach standing alone.

As Director of your Management and Quality Training program, I will
successfully lead your staff members to **challenge** the traditional *"not
my job"* orientation. Instead they will:

- **Adopt a broad view,** questioning and looking beyond existing
  methods of operating, in order to invest in the future.

- **Raise the overall level of their commitment** (despite setbacks,
  lack of support, and the passage of time) through the creation
  and nourishment of a **vision of quality.**

The rewards are profound. The process is painless when you have the
proper training and commitment at the helm. Let's get together so that
we can discuss this in person. I will call you shortly.

*Forceful
tone
matches
position.*

Sincerely,

Samuel H. Wong
Work: (555) 765-4321
Home: (555) 456-7890

Mr. Hugh Nichols
President
Panache Frozen Yogurt
410 Wymont Road
Long Island City, NY 09876

Dear Mr. Nichols:

Welcome to the neighborhood! Your move to White Plains from Long Island will introduce your staff to a superb location full of exceptional people -- many of whom, in today's economic climate, may be available to put their expertise to work for you.

How will you find the best that this new area has to offer? What Westchester publications will prove the most cost-effective for your recruiting advertisements? What area headhunters and search firms are the most reliable? Will your best on-staff recruiters be immediately available to interview in White Plains? How much will it cost you to bring them in from Long Island, or send your candidates out there for meetings?

The answer to all these questions is the same:

> **You'll save time and money by relying on a recruitment professional with solid experience, expertise, and contacts already in place right here in Westchester.**

As the enclosed resumé illustrates, I have 12 years of recruiting background, much of it in this area -- and I can put this to work for Panache immediately. Whether on a consultant, part- or full-time basis, I can serve as a valuable resource to help you get your new facility up and running as quickly as possible.

With the most qualified people.
With minimum delay or misspent dollars.
With maximum results.

Let's get together to discuss the difference I can make to your start-up time. I'll give you a call to see if there's a convenient time for us to meet. Or please feel free to call me at (555) 345-6789.

Sincerely,

Ricardo L. Munoz

Timely opening

Dr. Louis Dresser-Smythe
Director of Administration
State University
St. Albans, VT 09876

RE: Director of Human Resources and Administrative Services

Dear Dr. Dresser-Smythe:

The position described in your advertisement seems to have been written for me. I possess the precise qualifications you seek, and have been searching for just this opportunity to apply my business background to academic life.

Allow me to elaborate on the enclosed resumé to demonstrate the strengths I can bring to your institution.

Human Resources Expertise: My employee relations responsibilities have made me skilled at conflict resolution, staffing, development, and personal counseling. For administrative hiring and staff recruiting, I develop position profiles, direct and provide input for employee evaluations and compensation, supervise training and benefits administration, ensure legal compliance and advance policy.

Administrative Expertise: Acting as the *de facto* Director of Administration, I supervise office and facilities services, marketing administration, and the research library. Because I have successfully directed projects involving the structuring and implementation of a library catalogue, office redesign, equipment planning and acquisition, marketing database design, and planning a newsletter series, I can spearhead these and other initiatives on your behalf.

Exceptional Written Communication Skills: My ongoing work creating policy statements, project summaries, and correspondence for myself and the company's senior management provides you with a valuable on-staff resource.

Throughout my successful career, I have maintained my connection to academia through my graduate studies in the sociology of education. The university environment is one in which I am well-versed, challenged, and entirely comfortable.

I would welcome the opportunity to apply my skills and expertise in an academic setting such as yours. I offer you, in return, a colleague with the focus and ability to perform effectively under pressure -- talents refined through 12 years in a fast-paced corporate setting.

Sincerely,

B. Martha Gordon
(555) 456-7890 work

Mr. Jonathan Bates
Americana Corporation
9500 Corporate Drive
Detroit, Michigan 09876

Dear Mr. Bates:

The fact that you have advertised for a Quality Management Director (City Times, January 5) demonstrates your commitment to realign the corporate culture. It is this same commitment that has defined my career.

Indeed, over the past 25 years in corporate training and human resource development, my focus has been on supporting innovation and leadership -- on designing rather than adapting to the future.

I am certain that my past achievements augur similar productivity improvements for Americana. For example, I have led corporate management teams to:

-Commit themselves entirely to the goal of superior quality in every aspect of service and performance.

-Drive this commitment into every level of the organization's culture and operations so that it becomes the everyday way of working.

-Free managers from their traditional focus on authority and control so that they can embrace critical leadership ideals.

-Build these transformations into an existing infrastructure, thus avoiding costly and time-consuming changes that erode success.

Undoubtedly, these are the objectives you seek to realize at Americana -- and I would consider it a privilege to explore them further with you. I feel certain that my background and expertise (described in detail on the enclosed resumé) would be a singular asset to your organization.

I can be reached at (555) 456-7890.

Sincerely,

T. Wilson Johanson

Mr. Abraham Silver
President
U.S. Manufacturing Corporation
23-34 Winton Way
Madison, WI 09876

Dear Mr. Silver:

In your search for a Director of Productivity Improvement, you are focusing on, fostering, generating, expanding, and repeating results. *But first you have to find someone who has achieved them.*

My resumé presents my background and qualifications. Allow me to introduce myself via the results I have achieved. In the '80s at Eagle Steel, and now at DVC Equipment, I designed and implemented programs to foster breakthrough thinking. Learning to turn everyday obstacles and interruptions into innovation and success, our task teams:

-Increased both short- and long-term ROI by more than 38%.

-Improved cross-functional and cross-organizational teamwork by distinguishing *interpretation* from *fact* in order to take decisive actions.

-Realized quantum leaps in productivity performance, exceeding 80% in some cases, that went well beyond typical incremental improvements.

These are real, measurable, and profitable results. And they are reproducible at U.S. Manufacturing.

I'd like very much to meet with you in person. Please give me a call at (555) 765-4321. I'll alert my assistant to put your call through at once.

Best regards,

Jennifer Forsythe

Dr. Andrew Milhouse, President
The State University at Aurora
Campus Circle
Aurora, SC 09876

Dear Dr. Milhouse:

$500 million is not the most. It's the <u>average</u> amount of money my fund raising programs have generated for hospitals, private secondary schools, government programs, colleges, and universities.

Killer opening!

This figure, attained through 22 years of intensive fund raising experience, equips me to assume the responsibilities of Aurora's Director of Development as rapidly and effectively as your needs demand.

I have enclosed summaries of my background and those projects that are most germane to your situation. As you'll see, I have regularly built the coalitions of citizens, alumni, business and community leaders with the power to make significant contributions, and to attract major funding from others.

My success at The Broderick Group has been enormously gratifying. However, I am eager to sacrifice the rigors of city life for the pleasures of the country and academia, an environment I enjoyed years ago as a Professor of Economics.

Rather than let my credentials speak for themselves, I would enjoy meeting with you in person. Business frequently brings me to your area so I will call you shortly to schedule an appointment.

With best regards,

Beth Daniels
(555) 456-7890

Enclosures

A clever approach, appropriate for the industry and position, definitely attracts attention.

Ms. Regina Lin, President
UniFex Corporation
18 Southern Parkway
Miami, Florida 09876

RE: Your Ad for a CFO

Dear Ms. Lin:

You're looking at an actual demonstration of the results I can produce for you. At PSB, I've **expanded profit margins to 70%.** How? By cutting the cost of purchased goods by up to 25%. By cutting the cost of purchased services by up to 38%. By rigorously examining every expenditure to ensure maximum value at minimum cost. So why not hire me to do for UniFex what I do best? **I increase margins.** In fact, as you can see, I can't resist expanding any margin I can get my hands on.

Sincerely,

Richard C. Royce
(555) 456-7890

Resumé enclosed

Ms. Dianne Williams, President
TWI International   RE: Your ad for a CFO
850 North Delaware Avenue   City Times, May 5, 199X
Philadelphia, PA 09876

Dear Ms. Williams:

Yes, a Chief Financial Officer must be an expert in cash flow planning and management, financial accounting, the preparation of tax statements, inventory pricing, contract negotiations, sales, and profitability projections -- and I am.

But the *superior* CFO has also produced the following results -- as I have:

> -Completely restructured business liability insurance to reduce costs by 15% and increase coverage.

> -Solicited, selected, and managed a major lending bank to design cash management sweep/credit link to maximize overnight investment returns.

> -Cultivated a reliable source of nonbank capital to discount current accounts receivable to finance the acquisition of additional inventory.

This is simply an overview of my most recent accomplishments. It should demonstrate the commitment I make to cost control and heightened return.

Yes, I am currently employed and would appreciate your confidentiality when contacting me. But I will make myself available to meet at your convenience.

Sincerely,

E. Darrell Brighton-Fisk
(555) 456-7890 office
(555) 765-4321 home

4-117: EXECUTIVE SECRETARY—LANGUAGE ABILITY (COMPOSITE LETTER)

With minor changes, this letter has been fashioned from relevant paragraphs appearing in several other letters. It is now an ideal fit for an Executive Secretary applying to a firm that deals with an international clientele.

Name, Title
Company Name
Company Address
City, State ZIP

RE: Your __(date)__ ad
in the _(publication)_
for a __(position)__

Dear Mr./Ms. (Name):

To meet the extensive qualifications listed in your advertisement, a candidate must be a true professional with in-depth experience at a major corporation who is looking for an exciting new challenge. As I am.

This first paragraph is taken from Letter 4-25.

You'll find my resumé enclosed with this letter. Allow me to present the highlights here:

Superior dictaphone skills, steno at 100 words per minute, typing at 60 words per minute on a typewriter, faster with word processing such as …

… Microsoft Word for Windows, AmiPro and Lotus 1-2-3, all of which I have mastered (along with a basic knowledge of Excel and WordPerfect) through …

… __ years at _____ and __ years at a law firm, specializing in medical malpractice, which accounts for my …

… professionalism in dealing with the public, attorneys, physicians, emotional clients and the media …

… as well as my experience making travel arrangements for overworked lawyers who wish to escape all this!

This entire section is taken from Letter 4-24.

Furthermore, I am fluent in French, with fair skill in German, having been raised in a multicultural family. These language abilities will help you in dealing with international customers and prospects, as will my familiarity with foreign customs and protocol.

This paragraph is taken from Letter 4-23.

I would welcome the opportunity to discuss with you the numerous benefits my background could provide to __(Company Name)__. Let's get together to explore the possibilities. I will contact you to schedule an appointment.

The close is from Letter 4-59.

Sincerely,

Name
Telephone

This letter has been tailored from several others to focus more precisely on what a *recruiter* needs to know in order to successfully place this marketing pro.

Name, Title
Company Name
Company Address
City, State ZIP

Dear Mr./Ms. (Name):

I appreciate your willingness to assist in my job search. As promised, I have enclosed my resumé to provide background on my professional experience. To bring my resumé to life for you, allow me to tell you more about myself, and what sets me apart from other candidates against whom I may compete.

Opening from Letter 4-11

You see, through my tenure at two advertising agencies, I've been exposed to every facet of the marketing and advertising process. As I have for Fortune 500 companies and TelNet, a growing long-distance telecommunications firm, I can help your clients develop sound marketing strategies, innovative ad campaigns, targeted direct response programs, and a wealth of original promotional activities.

From Letter 4-33

My current involvement in the **development of innovative consumer product lines** will be of value to your clients. I have been personally instrumental in engineering successful promotional programs that produced annual sales well over **$3 million** each.

From Letter 4-49

These are the skills that define the successful Marketing Associate in any industry. I offer them to your clients -- along with my in-depth experience in strategic planning for retail, commercial, and business-to-business advertising.

From Letter 4-41

I would welcome the opportunity to meet with you. If you will call or leave a message on my home answering machine, I will return your call promptly.

Close from Letter 4-29

Sincerely,

Name
Telephone

4-119: COMPUTER MIS (COMPOSITE LETTER)

This letter has been adapted for the computer expert who wishes to let more of her personality shine through in a cover letter.

Name
Title
Company Name
Company Address
City, State ZIP

Dear Mr./Ms. (Name):

If your advertisement in the <u>City Times</u> was written to attract my attention, it worked like a charm!

Opening from Letter 4-49

Over the years, I have developed a reputation for introducing fresh approaches to solve the challenges faced in today's competitive business world. Because this is a personality trait -- not a learned skill -- it is one I can offer your firm with confidence. It is who I am. It has defined the contributions I have made in every position I have held.

From Letter 4-5

As my resumé illustrates, I possess the track record, technical knowledge, and expertise to effectively:

- Design, develop, implement, and support all MIS functions.

- Evaluate, recommend, and purchase hardware, software, and supplies.

- Manage, develop, and support multiplatform environments.

- Demonstrate proficiency with Appletalk, Novell, and Windows.

From Letter 4-75

When we meet, you'll find me to be a person with a positive outlook who enjoys identifying ways to make something work rather than reasons not to try. This perspective is invaluable in setting an example for employees who are called upon to assume numerous responsibilities -- of particular merit in this era of unavoidable downsizing and cost cutting.

From Letter 4-8

If these are the qualities you seek, I hope you will contact me. I will be happy to visit your office for an interview, at your convenience.

Close from Letter 4-94

Sincerely,

Name
Telephone

4-120: RELOCATING SENIOR EXECUTIVE (COMPOSITE LETTER)

This letter blends key points from five others to suit a relocating Senior Executive's specific talents and accomplishments.

Name, Title
Company Name
Company Address
City, State ZIP

Dear Mr./Ms. (Name):

Because I have long admired your achievement in building a successful company, I was dismayed to learn of your recent layoffs. In today's economy, such a situation presents the vexing conundrum: how to maximize opportunities for growth with diminished human resources?

Opening from Letter 4-8

> To move forward powerfully, effectively, and rapidly, today's employees must align themselves with common goals and with common ways to achieve these goals.

The next two paragraphs are from Letter 4-109.

Invariably, in promoting the concept of goal-oriented performance management, the organizations with which I have worked were pleased to discover that what's missing in many other quality initiatives is precisely what I have learned in over 16 years of building high-performance teams. I have *combined* my methodology with the tools of quality and process management to create a synergy that is far superior to either approach standing alone.

This background arms me to lead a firm such as yours in generating results as impressive as those I helped my current organization achieve:

This section is from Letter 4-78.

-Margins surpassing industry averages by 23%.

-Operations productivity 45% over previous levels.

-Domestic market share growth exceeding 30%.

Having recently engineered the downsizing of our business-to-business Marketing Services area, I am now anxious to apply my expertise to situations in which the pace of growth and opportunity represents more of a challenge.

From Letters 4-43 and 4-44

I will be relocating to the Seattle area shortly. It would be a privilege to meet with you personally to discuss the opportunity to add to your team. I will follow up by calling you soon to schedule an appointment.

Adapted from Letter 4-68

Sincerely,

Name
Telephone

This letter has been customized to reflect both the personality and background of this sales executive.

Name, Title
Company Name
Company Address
City, State ZIP

Dear Mr./Ms. (Name):

Your advertisement addresses my qualifications so ideally, one would think we've met. And we should -- because I can offer you the precise skills for which you're searching.

Opening from Letter 4-76

As you'll see on the enclosed resumé, the depth of my experience in sales offers you the opportunity to hire a real pro who needs little or no training, and is comfortable and successful with cold canvassing.

From Letter 4-46

Solid sales experience is only the first of my qualifications -- I have a successful track record and the recommendations to back it up.

From Letter 4-48

Proven ability to translate consumer desires into purchase decisions is only the second of my qualifications -- I have sold effectively within religious, upscale, and ethnic markets.

Superior customer service delivery is only the third qualification I possess -- I project warmth, enthusiasm, and a pleasant attitude.

In addition, I am able to work effectively and independently in the field without requiring costly, time-consuming supervision. Perhaps most importantly, I have developed strong presentation and sales closing skills that I can put to work immediately with the solid base of contacts I will bring to your organization.

The last two paragraphs are adapted from Letter 4-42.

My resumé, which is enclosed, details my career, accomplishments, and my education (BA in Economics/MBA.) I would be pleased to discuss my qualifications and salary/commission requirements in greater detail when we meet in person.

Sincerely,

Name
Telephone

Chapter 5

The Follow-Up Letter

Before reading any further, it's imperative to understand the distinction between the Follow-Up Letter, which is covered in *this* chapter and the Thank-You Letter, which is covered in the *following* chapter. In a Thank-You Letter your *sole* purpose for writing is to express appreciation. In the Follow-Up Letter your "thank-you" is only an *excuse* for writing to those who have the power either to hire you or to influence the hiring decision in your favor.

In this chapter, we focus on the Follow-Up Letter, the letter you write after being interviewed for a position that you are interested in attaining. Although you may begin your Follow-Up Letter by thanking your reader for a meeting, advice, a referral, or for consideration, your *Primary Goal* is to continue promoting yourself and your candidacy. You accomplish this by achieving your *Secondary Goal,* which is to strengthen a connection with your reader that you established during an interview, meeting, or other prior contact.

When should you send a Follow-Up Letter after interviewing for a position in which you are interested? Always. When should you send the same person another Follow-Up Letter after interviewing a second time for a position in which you are interested? Always. When should you send a Follow-Up Letter after receiving help from someone who can influence the hiring decision? Always.

You'll find Follow-Up Letters easy to draft if you follow these steps.

STEP 1: RE-ESTABLISH THE CONNECTION

Open your letter by mentioning something that will identify yourself to your reader, such as the time or place of the meeting. Because it's likely that your prospective employer met with numerous candidates, it's vital that she remembers you. If your meeting occurred early on in the hiring process, it's even more critical that your interviewer remembers you. And it's vital that her memory of you is a positive one.

Therefore, in your opening refer to a common link that was revealed during your meeting. You may have discovered, for example, that you and your interviewer both worked at the same company in the past, or that you share an alma mater, professional association, or business philosophy. Such a connection subtly suggests that you and your prospective employer are similar in some way, and will find common ground on which to build a rapport. (Unless you're planning to

179

work for Scrooge himself, it's a sure bet that your next boss will be searching for someone with whom he can get along on a daily basis.)

If there is no apparent connection of this type, refer to an unusual topic you discussed with your interviewer, or something you believe may be of interest or importance to whomever you're writing.

Sample Openings

- I enjoyed our lunch at the River Club and I thank you for your interest in me.
- It was a pleasure meeting you on Monday, and I appreciate the time you spent with me.
- Our meeting last week was very valuable for me, and I appreciate your willingness to fit me into your busy schedule.
- It was a pleasure meeting you again yesterday to discuss the opening in your media department. I especially appreciate your willingness to meet me so early in the morning.
- Thank you for your time last Friday. It was a pleasure discussing the plans you've conceived for your sales team, and I would welcome the opportunity to develop new business for your division.
- Meeting with you Tuesday morning was invaluable to me. It was rewarding to discover that a fellow U.S. Iron veteran has penetrated the upper echelons of our industry. Working with you would be a privilege.
- Thank you for your time at our breakfast on the 14th. I enjoyed meeting you, and swapping mountain bike trail secrets. Perhaps our paths will cross on Mt. Boulder; I certainly hope they will cross in business.
- I appreciate the time you spent with me on the 26th, and the information you provided on Data International's growth strategies. It was heartening to learn that we share the same excitement regarding the future of our industry, a future in which I hope to play an important role.
- Thank you for your time this past Wednesday morning. I enjoyed

meeting with you again and com-paring HydroMat stories. Our combined experiences certainly represent the good, the bad, and the ugly!

- I am grateful to you for introducing me to your colleagues. Meeting Mr. Simon and Ms. Weiss has only en-hanced my desire to put my strengths to work on your behalf. I would be thrilled to join the im-pressive legal team you've built.

- Thank you for introducing me to Jim Williams. As you predicted, he offered me a wealth of advice. I'm grateful for his perspective and for your interest.

STEP 2: INFORM

You may notice that this step is the same as Step 2 in your Resumé Cover Letters. That's because in both situations, your letter is dedicated to promoting your can-didacy. To do so, you must sell your strengths as well as the benefits they will bring your next employer.

In the body of your letter, remind your reader of the skills or knowledge you possess that make you perfectly suited to fill the open position. But don't stop with that—as your competition will.

Link these qualities to the meaningful advantages they offer your next boss and her company. To do this, think of your unique attributes as they fall under four categories: profits, productivity, performance, or personal satisfaction. Ask yourself how you can contribute to the success of the firm, a specific division, a team of people, or your immediate supervisor. Will your skills help to enhance productivity? Will your achievements play a role in increasing profits? Will you add to or improve performance? Will your personal satisfaction contribute in some way such as boosting morale, setting an example, introducing new ideas or a new perspective? You'll find that the most important benefits you can deliver will involve one or more of these areas.

In the body of your Follow-Up Letter you might also supply additional ref-erences or more detailed information on your skills. You might clarify or strength-en comments made during an interview.

181

If you are attempting to overcome a problem raised in your interview, provide a clear explanation with valid support points—not excuses! A good illustration is provided in Follow-Up Letter 5-1. In this case, the writer travelled to Denver to interview for a position in which she was very interested. Later, thinking back on the meeting, she became discouraged. Although she was more than willing to relocate for the job, she worried that her interviewer may have regarded the fact that she was from out of town as a drawback—a problem she did not perceive or address at the time. Instead of giving up, she responded with significant assurances that she could relocate successfully, building contacts and business relationships as she has before.

5-1: FOLLOW-UP LETTER—INSURANCE SALES

Mr. Howard Walsh
Sales Manager
Long Life Insurance Company
100 South College Boulevard
Denver, CO 80300

Dear Mr. Walsh:

Thank you for spending so much time with me during my visit to your headquarters on Monday.

Seeing the respect evident between you and your colleagues was completely refreshing for me -- as was discovering the innovative sales strategies you've introduced. I am eager to join forces with you.

You can count on me to quickly become a familiar face to prospects, clients, and business leaders in and around Denver. Through previous moves, I have become adept at forging contacts and friendships through my personal interest in the arts as well as my participation in the activities of local business groups (such as the Lifers Club, United Way, Police Athletic League, Financial Marketing Association, Advertising Club and the Red Cross in Atlanta). Turning these connections into sales is integral to my status as the top biller at my agency for four years running.

Dispels concerns raised during interview.

I will forward additional information to you shortly to support what my record has already proven: that I will produce nothing less than outstanding results for you and Long Life.

Sincerely,

Allison Deal
(555) 456-7890

STEP 3: INSTRUCT

In many cases, you will benefit from adding a reference to the next step in the hiring process—even if it's simply that you will wait to be contacted. Putting down on paper what will happen next, as you understand it, may help avoid misunderstandings about whose "court the ball is in."

If the next step will be his or hers, **tell the reader what to do.** Be sure to provide a complete address and telephone number at which you can be reached, stating whether the phone number is a work or home number. As you did in your Resumé Cover Letter, let your reader know if you prefer to be called during certain hours and if confidentiality is an issue.

If you will be the one to take the next step, **tell the reader what to expect.** You may make a general reference such as, "I'll call you shortly." Or you may be specific about what, when, and how you'll follow up: by phone, by mail, by express mail, by messenger. If you know that the hiring process has just begun, inform the reader that you'll call to follow up in two weeks, ten days, or whenever you feel it's appropriate.

Enclosing material with your letter always requires an explanation. Describe what the enclosure is: a resumé, a list of accomplishments, references.

If you will be sending something to the reader, such as a reference, state what it is and when you will do so.

OPTIONAL STEP 4: CLOSE WARMLY

In a business setting, it is perfectly acceptable to close your letter with a simple, straightforward "Sincerely."

RECRUITER'S TIP

THOROUGH FOLLOW-THROUGH

After an interview, follow-through on your part is critical. The person to whom you're writing may not scrutinize every word in your Follow-Up Letter, but he or she will surely notice that you've sent one—and be impressed that you did!

Plus, a good recruiter will expect to hear from you on the precise day you promised to follow up—so do. Without fail.

On some occasions, however, you may wish to use a more friendly sign-off. You might make a personal reference or mention something about the reader that suggests that he is not receiving a form letter, but rather a letter written specifically to him. If you are on a first-name basis with your reader, you might add the reader's name to your closing. A warm ending to your message makes you seem friendly and approachable, and indicates that you are the kind of person with whom most of us would prefer to work.

Too much warmth for the situation can sound unprofessional, though. As a rule, the degree of warmth you add should correspond with the number of times you've met your reader—without ever crossing the line by getting too personal or rude. Use your judgment, do what you feel comfortable with—but by all means, don't choose *not* to close your letter because you don't feel like writing a closing line.

Here are some sample closings for the Follow-Up Letter that may inspire you!

Sample Closings

- Thank you for your time and consideration.
- I appreciate your assistance.
- I thank you again for your time and candor. Let's talk again soon!
- Thank you for the opportunity to pursue the position of Research Director.
- I look forward to our next meeting.
- I look forward to seeing you again, Randy, on the tennis courts and at headquarters.
- I am eager to continue our discussions.
- My best wishes for your continued success in 199X.
- My best wishes for another successful quarter for your team.
- I would welcome the chance to work with you.
- Bill, I would consider it a privilege to join forces with you and hope to hear from you shortly.
- I would welcome the opportunity to contribute to your firm, and look forward to speaking with you soon.
- I have no doubt that my past success is a preview of what I can produce for you and MicroTech. I look forward to speaking with you soon.

Ms. Anne Rice
Constitution Savings Bank
3 Constitution Plaza
Miami, Florida 30330

Dear Ms. Rice:

Thank you for allowing me to present myself as a candidate for Operations Manager, a prospect about which I am very excited. It was a pleasure meeting you on Wednesday -- and discovering our mutual Midwestern roots!

Reaffirms connection ...

Given my background, I can understand the need for a Manager who can attend to detail without compromising the division's overall profitability. Throughout my tenure with Merrill Lynch, I have worked to achieve these demanding goals. During the past 10 years, <u>I personally led the division to cut costs by 12% while improving our overall accuracy rate to 98%.</u>

... informs by providing benefit meaningful to employer ...

What this means for you is that as Constitution's Operations Manager I can bring the same skill, insight, and experience to motivate your staff to improve accuracy, streamline costs, and increase the effectiveness of the "back room," bringing Operations to the forefront of the Bank's profit centers.

I will contact you shortly to see when we might meet again to expand upon this vital goal.

... instructs how next step will occur.

Sincerely,

Jim Williams
home (555) 456-7890

When her interview was interrupted, this writer continued it by telephone. She used this unique fact to remind the reader of their meeting and then continued with an upbeat tone.

Ms. Freida Gencliffe
Vice President
Gencliffe, Ackerman and Hahn
120 East Wacker Drive
Chicago, IL 09876

Dear Ms. Gencliffe:

I'm so pleased we were able to continue our discussions, even by phone, and I thank you for your time.

As you can tell, I am very excited about the opportunity to work with you and the top-notch team you've developed at Gencliffe, Ackerman and Hahn. I am particularly inspired by your belief in the value of promoting from within, which seems to be a rare insight these days. For this reason, and to provide further proof of the unique talents I can bring to your team, I have enclosed a summary of my recent case findings.

I am eager to prove my abilities and successes to you on a first-hand basis. I will keep in touch to see when we might meet again, and if there is any other information I can provide you in the meantime.

Thank you again for your time and consideration.

Sincerely,

Jamie Paksson

Ms. Elizabeth Porter
VisionQuest
3 Reading Way
Reading, PA 09876

Dear Ms. Porter:

Thank you for your time during our luncheon last week. My journey from
Conshohocken to Reading was a breeze, just as you predicted!

Aids recall.

VisionQuest's innovations are legendary among those "in the know," and it was
fascinating to discover the efforts that went into your unique achievements.
Those who benefit from your firm's breakthrough technologies in nonsurgical
visual impairment treatments cannot imagine the dedication and training
required of your teams.

I would welcome the opportunity to join a team such as yours and have,
therefore, enclosed a summary of my own accomplishments in research and
design. Because my procedures and standards of measurement are so similar
to those employed by VisionQuest, my assimilation with your team's
methodology would be quite smooth -- a breeze, in fact, like my trip to Reading!

Please let me know what additional information I can provide to help sway your
hiring decision in my direction.

I thank you again for your time.

Sincerely,

Alice DeNardo
(555) 456-7890 home
(555) 765-4321 work

Another example of ingenuity following an interrupted interview. Enclosing a photo is unusual ... exactly why it will attract attention!

Mr. Richard Clark
Vice President
The Prince Company
5 Prince Place
Albie, WY 09876

Dear Mr. Clark:

It was a pleasure meeting you during my visit to the Albie, and I look forward to the opportunity to continue our discussion.

After a delightful and very informative lunch with Susan Camelitto, I am tremendously excited by the prospect of working in the challenging and highly creative environment you've established at Prince. In return, I will bring you my proven strengths in research and new business development.

As our meeting was cut short, I have taken the liberty of enclosing my picture so that I'm clearly in your mind until we meet again, and I can convince you that I'm the ideal addition to your team.

Sincerely,

Matt Aspin
(555) 456-7890 work

Mr. Arthur Manning, President
Manning FiberOptics
Suite 900
111 Roosevelt Parkway
San Diego, CA 09876

Dear Arthur:

I want to thank you for your time on Wednesday. Our discussion left me even more excited about your sales team -- and convinced that I'd be a perfect fit.

As you know, I have dedicated the last 10 years of my career to electronic technologies. Now I'm eager to make that same commitment to a challenging growth business -- as Manning FiberOptics is.

Hire me and you'll get a loyal employee who is honest and hard working, and who understands the industry, clients, and buyers; someone with an established, solid reputation who will add to your image *and* your bottom line.

Arthur, I look forward to working with you to build big things together.

Sincerely,

Russell Brady

Ms. Tanya Russo
Director, Facilities Management
The Sunray Corporation
800 Magnolia Drive
Pensacola, FL 09876

Dear Ms. Russo:

I enjoyed our meeting last week and appreciate your time and candor. As another ex-IBMer, your perspective was especially meaningful to me.

Reaffirms connection.

My decade of experience in facilities management has made me a planner, a promoter, and a problem solver -- and it is a real pleasure to meet someone who values these qualities. Joining a division that recognizes and depends upon these strengths provides precisely the environment and challenge I seek.

In return, I offer you my <u>proven</u> track record in keeping costs under control while always getting more from agents than they had planned to offer. <u>Proven</u> by the fact that I have been IBM's leading site manager for the past 3 years, and will use my superiors as references!

I'd welcome the opportunity to work with you. I'll be in contact to see how we can make this happen.

Sincerely,

Voilet Nance Murray

The Case of the Poor Interviewer: Although this candidate could tell that the employer was impressed with her qualifications, she also surmised that he didn't know how to best make use of her skills. So she gives him several ideas.

Mr. Walter Muhdi
NetworCorp
1500 North First Street
Suite 4400
Salt Lake City, UT 09876

Dear Mr. Muhdi:

Thank you for the time you so generously spent with me this afternoon.

Now that I know so much more about NetworCorp's varied activities, I am even more eager to be a part of the company's future. Certainly, your firm and I both thrive on creativity, innovation, the energy of the entrepreneur and of the deal maker.

For this reason, as I mentioned during our meeting, I hope that you will think of me should an opportunity arise. Whether it be sales or marketing, dealing with the largest advertisers or new business development, working abroad or as your right-hand man, I would welcome the chance to work with you.

I thank you again for your time and consideration.

Sincerely,

Damon P. Silhousky
(555) 456-7890

Mr. Randolph Charles, Vice President
National Safety Systems, Inc.
26 East Ontario Street
Chicago, IL 09876

Dear Mr. Charles:

It was a pleasure speaking with you recently about your plans to expand into the corporate market.

I have just returned from two weeks vacation and am anxious to pursue our discussion of the exciting profit potential such a program can offer National Safety -- a potential of which I am well aware, having built Wytech Security's corporate program from the ground up to its current status as a major profit center for the company.

As a springboard for this discussion, I have enclosed another copy of my resumé. Since you last saw it, my responsibilities have been increased. I now lead the planning and implementation of one of the company's major strategic initiatives: promoting multisite security systems to firms that operate from coast to coast. I am responsible for the sale of full-service security system packages, which include customized system design, installation, and staff training.

As a result, I can offer National Safety Systems the experience, foresight, and personal contacts required to tap the corporate security market and to take full advantage of the potential for return this market offers.

I will contact you again shortly to see how we might proceed. I thank you again for your consideration and look forward to seeing you.

Sincerely,

A. Michael Greer
(555) 456-7890 work
(555) 765-4321 home

This aspiring actor called to confirm the agency's address and followed up with this letter. The agency sent him on numerous auditions, where he landed work in several print advertisements.

Ms. Jane S. McManus
McManus Model Management, Inc.
5200 Meredith Parkway
Suite 2424
Cinema City, CA 09876

Dear Ms. McManus:

In follow-up to my recent telephone conversation with your office, I am enclosing my headshots. As you'll see, I am a fresh face on the market.

I have the ideal look for a father, businessman, or active outdoors type in the 36 to 42 age range. I have recently completed The Model Market's commercial print course and have acquired the skills to compete effectively for bookings, and perform professionally on the set.

I will telephone you shortly to set up an appointment so that we may discuss opportunities that may arise through your agency.

I thank you in advance for your consideration.

Sincerely,

Thomas Williams
555-765-4321 (service)

Headshots enclosed

Ms. June Ellis-Parker
Grummond Associates
101 Alden Terrace
Ames, IA 09876

Dear Ms. Ellis-Parker:

Meeting you today was a real pleasure. I enjoyed touring your facility and seeing a staff that does not require formal attire to achieve impressive productivity. Quite a departure from the typical corporate environment!

As we discussed, the position is an exciting one for which I am superbly qualified, and it would be an honor to join your team. The range of skills I can bring to your organization would allow your managers to devote more time to joint field work, and ultimately increase your bottom line profits.

Employer benefits

I will call on Friday as you suggested to see whether Roger Transwood has returned and is available to meet with me.

Thank you again for your time. I look forward to seeing you again very soon.

Sincerely,

Linda Blumfeld
(555) 456-7890

Ms. Erica Magni
Brigham Products, Inc.
6534 Laudley Way
White Plains, NY 09876

Dear Ms. Magni:

Thank you for speaking with me at the recent State Collegiate Career Fair. Our conversation made a striking impression on me, and I appreciate your interest and encouragement.

As we discussed, I have enclosed my resumé as a follow-up to our discussion. Allow me to provide this brief overview of what I can offer your firm:

Leadership: Student Government Vice President, Sorority President, Big Sister Volunteer while maintaining a 3.5 GPA.

Interpersonal Strengths: I am pleased to report that my colleagues describe me as a go-getter who is reliable, pleasant, encouraging, and loyal.

Drive: I will be available to begin work immediately upon receiving my BS in Business Administration this spring from State University.

I will be in the area again next month, and will call to set up an appointment. In the meantime, I thank you again for your time at the Career Fair, and look forward to meeting you again soon.

Sincerely,

Brian Fogarty
Telephone at School: (555) 456-7890
Local Telephone: (555) 765-4321

Ms. Julia Klemperer, Comptroller
Howard Industries
Suite 300
67 Houston Street
Spring City, TX 09876

Dear Ms. Klemperer:

Thank you for the opportunity to meet you and interview for the Bookkeeper position. Hearing you recount the growth your company has enjoyed, I am certain that your own hard work and commitment are the roots of your success.

As your bookkeeper, I will bring the same dedication to the fulfillment of your firm's accounting responsibilities.

- I am adept at handling all aspects of your accounts payable, accounts receivable, payroll, and payroll taxes. My 5 years of experience in these areas means that you can rely on me for skill and accuracy.

- Unlike others in my field, I am well versed in handling a payroll with diverse commissions/bonus structures. This reduces or eliminates the potential for problems that arise when payment errors aggravate your Sales Representatives.

- Furthermore, my computer expertise (Peachtree, MAS90, and Quickbooks for MAC) allow me to contribute immediately, without taking valuable company time for training.

I would very much like to join your firm. If you require any additional information before making your decision, please let me know. I would be pleased to visit your office again for another meeting or provide further references, if you wish.

Thank you for considering me.

Sincerely,

Barton Hennessey
(555) 765-4321

In her interview, this candidate picked up on the importance her prospective boss placed on a single qualification: the ability to deal with difficult people. She focused on this here, even providing additional references to support her claim.

Mr. Wesley Valentin
Valentin Designs
1515 Severth Avenue
New York, NY 09876

Dear Mr. Valentin:

It was wonderful speaking with you last week. Thank you for spending so much time with me.

I am extremely interested in pursuing the Assistant Buyer opening at your firm because it represents the perfect match between your needs and my strengths.

My retailing background has familiarized me with an industry where diplomacy and tact are of supreme importance. As we discussed, the ability to quickly assess an individual in order to respond appropriately and productively is more a personality trait than an acquired skill -- it can rarely be taught.

I am pleased to report that my colleagues have repeatedly acknowledged my abilities in interpersonal communications. In fact, I have taken the liberty of enclosing several letters of referral that highlight this unique trait.

Great idea!

I hope it is evident that I would welcome the chance to work for Valentin Designs with you personally, Mr. Valentin. Please let me know if there is any further information you require.

Sincerely,

Rachael Isserman
(555) 456-7890 Telephone

Like its predecessor, the Cover Letter 4-85, this letter is heartfelt and sincere, yet still informative—very effective.

Ms. Leonore Valerio
Lincoln Center Institute
New York, NY 09876

Dear Ms. Valerio:

Thank you for taking an interest in me as a teaching artist for Lincoln Center. I enjoyed our telephone conversation of last week, and have received the information you forwarded to me.

This position represents an important opportunity for me to continue my productive association with the Lincoln Center Institute. As both a dancer and dance captain with LCI, I meet regularly with the artists prior to our performances to explore the link between the classroom material and the post-performance open talk. Invariably, this preparation proves priceless to students who benefit from a newfound familiarity with the elements of dance, and the terminology introduced in class.

This, along with my current participation as a member of your affiliated New York City Baroque Dance Company, reinforces my teaching philosophy: to share with my students the great joy of movement. I have found that every student can experience the pleasures of dancing, and of learning about the many methods for expression through movement. Depending upon their age and level, I introduce my students to various technical challenges, dance forms, and elements of composition. With the advantage of live performance, which your program offers, a teacher can guide the students towards a better understanding and appreciation of the performing arts. Books, pictures, and video tapes can enhance, but not replace, the experience of a live performance -- and the students truly enjoy it!

As an artist, I believe we have an obligation to show society the ways in which art can be brought into the mainstream of education. As a mother, I understand that a child's intellectual and emotional development must be well-rounded. I feel strongly that we can allow neither the winds of politics nor families' failings to adversely affect an entire new generation. Plus, we owe it to our future artists to help create a society supportive of the arts, one in which the arts may flourish.

Combined, my experience and commitment offer the advantages only a dedicated artist and educator can offer. I would appreciate the opportunity to meet with you personally. I salute the wonderful LCI program, and thank you again for your consideration.

Sincerely,

Isadora Ilianya

Ms. Chikara Itano
Denson & Denson Chemicals
1490 Anaheim Way
Anaheim, FL 09876

Dear Ms. Itano:

Congratulations on your promotion! It's so gratifying to see women recognized for their skills.

I enjoyed speaking with you on the phone yesterday, and, as promised, I've enclosed some information on myself and my capabilities. As you'll see, I've had a fair amount of experience within the financial services arena as well as a pseudomedical education.

My particular expertise is in the pharmaceuticals industry, a field in which many writers are less fluent. I am well-versed in the chemical and medical "lingo" that supports a vast range of pediatric, nutritional, pharmaceutical, and biological prescriptions, and over-the-counter products, as well as the government regulations governing their discussion in any public forum. This knowledge allows me to execute a greater number of projects at a far faster pace than other technical writers.

I would welcome the chance to show you samples of my work, at your convenience. When things settle down for both of us, let's get together. I will call you again towards the end of this month.

In the meantime, I wish you the best in your new position.

Sincerely,

Amy Rubenstein
(555) 456-7890

Mr. Harold Hancock
Vice President
Genebyte Technologies, Inc.
42-14 San Mateo Road
San Jose, CA 09876

Dear Hal:

It was great to see you yesterday and reminisce about our days at
Growth Systems. Seems like just yesterday -- but I digress!

Although I am chagrined that Genebyte's hiring freeze is still in place, I
do appreciate your offer to recommend me after the thaw. As you know,
our work at Growth Systems during those heady days when the computer industry was being born provides a background few can match. It
would be a thrill to join forces with you again -- especially on a project
as exciting as your multimedia/cellular assignment.

Hal, thanks again for seeing me and filling me in on Genebyte's
activities. Please give my regards to Jill.

I'll keep in touch.

Best,

Jim Dixon

Chapter 6

The Thank-You Letter

Note: Before you proceed any further into this chapter than this paragraph, be sure you are reading the appropriate material. The Thank-You Letter and the Follow-Up Letter are entirely different from each other. Each is written and sent under completely different circumstances. If you have just concluded an interview and wish to send a letter to further promote your candidacy, turn back to Chap. 5 for instructions on how to compose a Follow-Up Letter. If you wish to send a brief, yet sincere, note of appreciation—and have no hidden agenda—read on.

Thank-You Letters are honest and straightforward, with a simple, singular message. Your only reason for writing is to say "thank you," and nothing else. You may be expressing your gratitude to someone for an introduction, advice, a referral, or serving as a reference for you. You may have interviewed for a job, which you do not intend to pursue, but wish to thank your interviewer for seeing you.

These are the circumstances that occasion writing and sending a Thank-You Letter, and effective jobhunters never overlook them. In fact, you should actively seek opportunities to send Thank-You notes. The reason is simple: People like to be appreciated. Doing something for someone else involves going out of our way, and we feel (rightly) that we deserve acknowledgement for it. If we give nothing more than our time, we've given a great deal as time is, invariably, in short supply in the business world. When you satisfy this need to be appreciated, you help cement a positive image of yourself in your reader's mind—one that will serve you well should you ever approach this person with another request. And in today's complex, interactive business environment, you will. Not only are you

---

RECRUITER'S TIP

BERATE THE BELATED

Thank-you letters should be short, direct, and easier to compose than other jobhunting letters—so there's no excuse to delay sending them.

Always send your letter within one or two days of whatever occasion you're acknowledging.

If you can't meet this deadline, send one whenever you can, even weeks after the fact. It's never too late to thank someone for a kindness.

highly likely to have additional contact with your reader, but successful networking depends upon it. Do not miss an opportunity to send a thank-you note—you may be repaid with unexpected surprises later on!

At its most basic, a Thank-You Letter is an expression of feelings. These letters should be short and, contrary to popular belief, they are easy to write as long as you state your message simply. Your *Primary Goal* is to thank someone for her time, assistance, or support. You should have no *Secondary Goal*; if you do, it's likely that the letter you should be writing is a Follow-Up Letter (see Chap. 5) or a Make Something Happen Letter (see Chap. 7).

STEP 1: STATE THE OCCASION

Open your letter by referring to the occasion that inspired it. Tell the reader why you're writing. Be clear, direct, brief. A few examples follow; you'll find plenty more in every sample letter in this chapter.

Sample Openings

- Thank you for your time and advice.
- Thank you for seeing me yesterday.
- Your time and advice are most appreciated, and I thank you for meeting with me earlier this week.
- Knowing how busy you are at this time of year, I am grateful that you were able to make the time to meet with me this past Wednesday morning.
- Thank you for fitting me into your busy schedule. I appreciate the suggestions you made regarding my search for work and have already begun to contact the organizations we discussed.
- I appreciate your willingness to help me in my job search and thank you for passing my name along to your associates.
- Thank you for serving as a reference for me in my job search. Your contribution will certainly prove valuable as your name is so highly regarded in our field.
- Thank you for introducing me to Dr. Beatty. I appreciate your assistance and the referral to such an outstanding professional.

STEP 2: PROVIDE INFORMATION OR STATE YOUR FEELINGS

The body of your letter is the place to provide a bit of detail. This is where you'll tell your reader *how* his or her assistance was valuable to you.

Be specific about what you thank your readers for; if they don't know you personally, they may have already forgotten you! Make your thanks meaningful to the person who helped you—if positive, mention the results of that help and the difference it made in your job search. Say, for example, that a colleague recommended that you contact a Ms. Farrell. You called, scheduled a get-together, and gained important advice during the meeting. Because your colleague will want to know how you used the referral and how the meeting went, you might write:

> Meeting Ms. Farrell was invaluable to me. She shared with me her view of the future of endocrine therapy research, which in turn, led me to refine my job search strategy. As a result of our meeting, I will be contacting Stan Whitmore, an acquaintance of Ms. Farrell's, who directs product development for Pfizer Inc.'s pharmaceutical division.

Not only is it a courtesy to inform your colleague of the results of the referral, it's good networking. With the knowledge that you have properly handled the referral—and that Ms. Farrell found you impressive enough to further refer you to a colleague of hers—your friend will likely be willing to provide additional assistance in the future. (It should go without saying that the next letter you write will be to Ms. Farrell.)

If you choose not to go into this level of detail—for example, if the results were less than you expected—state your feelings instead of providing information. In this case, the rule is always: Say—don't describe—how you feel. Whether you're mildly grateful, very grateful, eternally grateful, or not at all grateful, this can be accomplished in very few words. Give the necessary information and STOP.

Your Thank-You Letters should always be brief, direct, and written with a positive tone of voice. Because they are short and easy to write, there's no excuse to avoid sending a Thank-You Letter. So don't pass on this chance to network! Use the sample letters provided on the following pages to guide you as you compose your own.

Ms. Irene Bernstein
Creative Director
Bruner and Bernstein Advertising
359 Madison Avenue
New York, NY 09876

Dear Ms. Bernstein:

Gracias! Merci! Danke schoen! Thank you! In any language, my appreciation is genuine. You gave me your time and your expert advice this past Tuesday, and I am very grateful.

States occasion.

You reassured me that despite tough times in the ad business, opportunities do exist for those willing to create them -- and nontraditional marketing seems to be a terrific place to start. Thanks to my experience in strategic planning and packaging, I am ideally equipped to identify and exploit new markets, especially on the international level.

How it helped

Your suggestion to contact Victor Morelli is much appreciated. I have just mailed him my resumé with hopes to discuss with him the overseas plans of Victory Advertising to which, I am certain, I can contribute fresh ideas, valuable experience, and strategic insight.

With sincerest thanks,

Mercedes H. Grulnord

Mr. Ivan Dreshniv
Delaware Job Corps
1223 Christiana Way
Wilmington, DE 09876

Dear Mr. Dreshniv:

Thank you for passing along my resumé to William Ford.

Mr. Ford has contacted me and we plan to meet on Tuesday, March 5. Our brief telephone conversation assures me that he will be a valuable resource in my job search.

I will call you next week to let you know the details of our meeting.

I appreciate your efforts on my behalf.

Sincerely,

Brain John Winakur

Ms. Joan Pozzi
Executive Recruiting Company
990 Madison Avenue
New York, NY 09876

Dear Ms. Pozzi:

Thank you for referring me to Bill Hancock at
Manhattan Legal Services.

Mr. Hancock called me today and we have scheduled a
meeting for next Wednesday, the 17th of April.

I couldn't have been more pleased when he indicated
that it was you who referred me to him. My sincerest
thanks for thinking of me, and making the time for
an introduction. You have become a valuable resource
in my job search, and I am grateful for all you have
done.

I will let you know the results of my meeting with
Mr. Hancock.

With best regards,

WIlliam P. Harmon, III

Mr. Victor Hernandez
American Products, Inc.
427 Claremont
San Antonio, TX 09876

Dear Mr. Hernandez:

Thank you for your time and interest during our meeting last week. American Products' planned expansion into European and Russian markets is as fascinating as it is challenging.

While the opportunity to participate in this exciting new venture is extremely appealing, I must, unfortunately, withdraw my name from consideration. I had hoped to be able to accept an international assignment, and have only recently been offered additional responsibilities in my current position, which will also involve limited travel overseas.

Nonetheless, I want to thank you for allowing me to explore what promises to be a career-making opportunity for the executive fortunate enough to be selected.

Meeting you was a pleasure, and I will stay in touch. My best wishes for your continued success.

All the best,

Myron Greenthal

Ms. Angela Terchetti
GNC, Inc.
1200 Lincoln Avenue
Atlanta, GA 09876

Dear Ms. Terchetti:

I have just returned from my second interview with Phyllis Anderson at Anderson, Wilton and Slatsky. She was thrilled with your comments about my performance during my tenure with you at DPC International -- and so am I!

As you know, I am anxious to further my career, and working with Ms. Anderson will supplement my experience in a meaningful and productive way.

I am so grateful to you for providing me with a positive recommendation. One day the opportunity will arise for me to repay your kindness, and you can be certain that I will be jumping to your side on that day.

In the meantime, with deepest thanks I am,

Nancy E. Alderson

This is a lovely thank-you note that sets the stage should Betty Anne decide to contact Mr. Fremont later in the networking process.

Mr. William Freemont
Freemont, Mason and Lazard
150 Avenue of Hope
Trallin, North Carolina 09876

Dear Mr. Freemont:

I cannot let another day pass without letting you know how very valuable I found your Jobhunting Seminar at North Carolina University last month. Your suggestions, ideas, and tips were very enlightening, and I have already put them to use in my job search.

Of greatest benefit for many of us was the motivation you instilled. Continuing the search can be especially daunting for students who compete against the hundreds of thousands of graduates flooding the market each spring, not to mention the many Americans already looking for work.

I shall remember your advice every day until I have successfully secured employment -- when I hope to have the chance to pass it along to other students graduating in the years to come.

Best regards,

Betty Anne Marville
North Carolina University Class of 199X
(555) 765-4321

Predating this contact with Professor Price, this jobhunter wrote him to ask whether or not he would serve as a reference for her. That letter appears in Chap. 8.

Professor James Price
Economics Department
State University
University City, MO 09876

Dear Professor Price:

I owe you dual thanks. First, for serving as a reference for me to aid in my job search and, second, for your kind words.

I have just heard from John Brunswick at St. Louis Federal, and Leslie Rubin at the South County Credit Union. They both informed me that you offered high praise of my work and my attitude.

As a result of your recommendations, I have been invited to join South County's training program. I should learn my status at St. Louis Federal shortly, and you can be certain that I will contact you as soon as I receive this decision.

So, for your dual role in my search, I thank you once, and I thank you again.

Fondly,

Jennifer Lawrence

Friends and family deserve recognition just as much as business colleagues do. The only difference is that a Thank-You Letter such as this one (which is written to the mother of a high school buddy) may be handwritten on personal notepaper, if you choose.

Mrs. Helen Gold
24 Oakwood Lane
Moorestown, NJ 09876

Dear Mrs. Gold,

Thank you for introducing me to your brother, Charles Armour. I spoke with his secretary just this morning and have scheduled a meeting for next Wednesday at his Maple Shade plant!

Armour Development has such a fine reputation in our area. I am looking forward to touring your brother's facilities, and gaining the benefit of any advice he may offer in my job search.

Mrs. Gold, it was so kind of you to help me. I truly appreciate your interest. Just as when Tom and I were playing football for the high school, you're still cheering us on! That support means a lot. Thank you.

Fondly,

Mark Reed

Ms. Miriam Goettel
Associate Publisher
Windy City News
404 State Street
Chicago, IL 09876

Dear Ms. Goettel:

Just a note to thank you for a most enjoyable early Monday morning meeting. It was nice meeting you and then seeing you again later at the CPG outing!

Now that I know more about *Windy City News*'s objectives and opportunities, I am excited about the newspaper's promise. I appreciate your willingness to have me meet the publisher, Frank Harley, a meeting I have arranged for next Wednesday.

Your offer to call with any questions that may arise is a kind one, and I will surely keep in touch. Thank you again for your interest.

Warm regards,

Philip E. Osterman

Mr. Adam Hyland
Hyland, Kincaid, Stern
8484 Soundview Drive
Bristol Beach, RI 09876

Dear Mr. Hyland:

It was a pleasure speaking with you on the phone last week.

I want to thank you for arranging for me to meet with Bill Stern on Monday, May 24 at 10:30 a.m. In preparation for this meeting, I am reviewing the Annual Report you sent me.

I am looking forward to meeting Mr. Stern and discovering more about Hyland, Kincaid, Stern.

Thank you again for your kind assistance.

Sincerely,

Moira O'Herlihy

Chapter 7

The Make Something Happen Letter

It never fails. You send in your resumé, schedule an interview, ace it, and then you wait … and wait … and wait. Who knows why? The firm might have hired another candidate without informing you (as rude as this is, it happens all the time). The hiring process may have been interrupted for any number of reasons: budget cuts, a hiring freeze, downsizing, the company was put up for sale. Your interviewer may be experiencing difficulty choosing from a strong field of candidates. Perhaps the person responsible for hiring has simply taken a three-week vacation.

Whatever the reason for the unnerving quiet, you should consider yourself a viable candidate until you hear otherwise. If you haven't heard anything, you haven't heard "No," so take advantage of the uncertainty. Whip out that pen, turn on that computer, and keep that motivation flowing. Try and get the hiring process moving in your direction. Writing and sending a well planned Make Something Happen Letter demonstrates your eagerness to work for the person or firm, *and* your ability to follow through on an endeavor to completion—both of which are impressive qualifications to most employers.

The Make Something Happen Letter is aptly named. Its purpose is to make something happen. It is meant to rev the hiring engines and to re-present yourself as a sterling candidate for the open position. This letter also helps to sway the decision maker's opinion away from your competition, and towards you. In writing this letter, your *Primary Goal* is to promote yourself. Your *Secondary Goal* is to jump start the hiring process. And with a little preparation, you can accomplish both simultaneously.

Before you begin to write, take a moment to reassess the situation. Be certain that you have not been rejected so graciously, in fact, that you may have misunderstood. Be sure that you are a viable candidate, with relevant skills and experience; if you are irrefutably unqualified, there may be little point in pushing now. Most importantly, try and discern whether the person to whom you're writing will be receptive to your assertiveness.

If you determine that you are a reasonable candidate and that an active, aggressive step is called for, the Make Something Happen Letter can often do the trick. If you're unsure but figure it's worth a shot, lessen the risk by matching the

214

tone of voice you use in your letter to that of your reader or the position you seek. Many of the sample letters that follow in this chapter involve sales positions, for which assertiveness is a desired quality; the letters reflect this trait in the tone the writers adopt.

STEP 1: GET TO THE POINT

No two Make Something Happen Letters are the same. Each relates specifically to the position you're after, the organization you'll be a part of when hired, the industry, the characters of those with whom you're dealing, and your own personality. Weigh each of these elements in your effort to create an appropriate opening for your letter.

A conservative industry, for example, might dictate the use of a reserved, understated tone. Or, a bolder approach might be effective in shaking things up a bit. Writing to an interviewer who appears to be all suit and wingtips, who would never dress down on a summer Friday, might call for a completely different opening than one you would use with a colleague you've known for years. You'll find examples of these and other openings in the sample letters that follow.

If your instinct has proven generally reliable in the past, you'll probably conjure up an opening that is clever, yet appropriate. If you're uncertain, adopt a more conservative approach. The bottom line, however, is to get to the point. Your opening should never require as much time to read as you have invested in planning it. Whether you're thanking your reader for a meeting, reminding him who you are, providing additional information or references, or asking for the job, get to the point. Then, move along to step 2.

STEP 2: MAKE THE POINT

A quick opening will direct your reader to the body of your letter, in which you'll make your central point (or points) clearly and concisely. In virtually every case, your Make Something Happen Letters will be brief.

Say something new in the body of your letter. There's no justification for repeating points you've already made during an interview or in a previous letter—evidently, they didn't work the first time. Instead, provide new information that is meaningful and beneficial to the reader. If appropriate, furnish additional references that might support your candidacy. Offer to spend more time with your prospective employer, particularly if you suspect that the decision maker is having trouble selecting from a field of strong candidates. Enclose a newspaper article that is germane to a topic discussed during your meeting. Inform your reader of a relevant event that occurred since you met such as a goal you achieved, an important sale you netted, an award you earned, or a project successfully completed.

If you genuinely can't come up with a single idea to add, try summarizing your qualifications in order to reinforce the fact that you meet all the employer's requirements.

Whatever you're reason for writing, state it succinctly. Remember that you're writing to get the hiring process moving, and not to bog it down further.

OPTIONAL STEP 3: THE KILLER CLOSE

As you review the sample letters that follow, you'll encounter a variety of different styles. The rule of thumb is this: the more forceful the letter, the more hard hitting the close. From the direct "Hire me" to the warm, polite "I hope all is well with you and look forward to seeing you soon," each letter reflects the specifics of that writer's situation and the players involved.

The assessment of your own situation that you make before beginning to write should carry you through to your close, if you choose to include one. Continue with the same tone of voice you've used throughout the letter. Changing your tone now will make you sound insincere.

Mr. Steve Pincus
Human Relations
Winfield Medical
100 Main Street
Winfield, FL 09876

Dear Mr. Pincus:

Our last discussion left me thoroughly convinced that I can produce dramatic results for Winfield Medical.

Strong opening

Count on my intelligence, experience, innate "people power," top-notch positioning, negotiation, and follow-up skills to bring in the steady stream of business you seek.

Hire someone with the know-how, the guts, and the goods to succeed. Hire someone as committed to performance as you are.

Hire me.

Sincerely,

Equally strong close

John Apgood
(555) 456-789 Home Phone
(555) 765-4321 Work Phone

To keep her name in front of the decision maker, this writer sends additional recommendations supporting her candidacy. Notice her tone of voice: positive, yet polite.

Ms. Melanie Orloff
Principal
Habingdon High School
Habingdon, ME 09876

Dear Ms. Orloff:

I had the pleasure of meeting with Marie Hammer last month regarding the opening in the Math Department at Habingdon High School. Because she suggested that you might be considering candidates at this time, I thought I would send you my most recent recommendations.

In May 199X I received my MA in Math Education from the University of Vermont where I was fortunate to have been selected to assist Dr. Michael Gutfreund with his research on the visual acquisition of math skills. Since then I have been teaching at Prescott South, and have thoroughly enjoyed my experience there.

Thank you for your time, Ms. Orloff. I would consider it a privilege to meet with you in person!

With regards,

Fredericka A. Drummond

Envisioning a tough selection choice, this candidate offers to meet again with the decison makers, and suggests an additional course of action even the employer may not have considered. Notice the creative visual approach.

Ms. Betty Maynard
PillowTek
400 Broadway
New York, NY 10101

Dear Ms. Maynard:

Now that we've met several times, you know more about me. For instance, you know that …

I am loyal and reliable.

I am willing to take on any project.

I see things through to completion.

I help my co-workers whenever I can.

<u>I want very much to work for you!</u>

Now that your hiring deadline is approaching, perhaps I can help make your selection easier. Please feel free to call me in at any time for another meeting. I would be happy to meet with others on your staff or to complete a sample assignment for you.

I look forward to hearing from you.

Sincerely,

Kevin P. Cast
(555) 456-7890

Ms. Annette Norcross
Sales Director
American Appliance, Inc.
100 Southern Boulevard
San Diego, California 09876

Dear Ms. Norcross:

No, I could not be more eager to join forces with you! Yes, as the new leader of your Sales team, I will use and foster effective sales skill like this: <u>follow through until the deal is closed</u>.

Unusual opener grabs attention.

That's why I'm writing you again -- to remind you of the uncommon benefits I will provide as your Sales Manager:

- The advantage of <u>existing</u> profitable relationships with decision makers at top retailers in all major markets.

- Unusual strength in perceiving industry trends and challenges, and translating them into sales opportunities -- well before others do.

- Proven ability to put these advantages to work for you from day one.

As you know Ms. Norcross, I am very anxious to work with you. Please let me know if I can help you make your selection by providing any further information or coming in for another interview. Feel free to call me at work or at home.

Sincerely,

Bill Dial
(555) 456-7890 home
(555) 765-4321 office

Instead of including them on his resumé, this jobhunter saved a listing of his accomplishments for just this purpose—to make something happen.

Ms. Alice B. Singleton
President
National Silk Company
2124-56 Wilton Avenue
Billingham, WA 09876

Dear Ms. Singleton:

Since my eye-opening and mouth-watering visit to your headquarters (thank you again for your time!) I've been fortunate to have resumed my conversation with Paul Salamone, which was sadly interrupted.

Along with the ones you and I had, this discussion fanned my desire to be a strong and vital part of your sales team.

For evidence of the experience and maturity I can offer you, you have only to look at the outstanding results I've produced in a variety of marketplaces under a variety of market conditions. But should you seek greater confirmation, I have enclosed an overview of my accomplishments in both sales and management, which I also sent to Mr. Salamone.

I have no doubt that these successes are but a preview of what I can produce for you and National Silk. I look forward to speaking with you soon.

Sincerely,

John M. Leventhal

Ms. Georgette Filamina
Vice President
Travel International
260 Madison Avenue
New York, NY 10016

Dear Georgette:

It was a pleasure meeting with you yesterday morning, and I thank you for your time.

I thought you'd be interested in the enclosed article, which I came across this morning, analyzing the public's reaction to the tranformation of the Soviet Union. It's the prospect of working with precisely this kind of challenge -- where attitudes can change rapidly and dramatically -- that is so <u>tremendously</u> exciting for me.

Good reason to write ... nice tie-in

If you're looking for proven results within both the traveling private and public sectors, success in and outside of New York, the innovation it takes to literally find money, and someone who can hit the ground running -- look no further. My expertise, interest, desire, and track record will fit perfectly.

I have always succeeded by finding or creating opportunities where others thought none existed; it's how I've become and remained top biller at Corporate Travel Inc., and it's what I will do for you.

Let's make it happen!

Sincerely,

Ruth Stella
(555) 456-7890

The length of this letter is justified by the strong and in-depth support points the jobhunter has included to overcome her interviewer's concerns.

Mr. Anton Revinsky, Director of Sales
Cable Information Systems, Inc.
400 Avenue of the Americas
New York, NY 09876

Dear Anton:

My meeting last week with you and Carol Keller has left me even more eager to work with you both, and the Cable Information Systems team. The more I ruminate, the more convinced I am that the match of your needs and my talents is an ideal one. I take the liberty of putting my thoughts on paper to reinforce our discussions!

I mentioned that when I joined WDEN-TV Sales, my list was by no means the largest at the station. I built it up to the top billing list and keep it there through concentrated effort, with exceptional organizational skills, and, most importantly, by finding new and better ways to serve the customer -- **as I will do for you.**

For example, I provide consistent, thorough service to my clients. When my clients invest in the station, it's a direct result of the TRUST they have in me. Not only do I accurately book a large volume of orders, but I regularly monitor their schedules to assure correct placement and rotations -- which also serves to limit discrepancies and ensure collections.

Plus, I serve as a valuable resource for my clients. My strong research background means that my sales technique goes well beyond selling numbers out of a rating book (at which I excel). To give current and potential clients more information and greater perspective, I take advantage of qualitative marketing tools such as trade publications, newspapers, and competitive information. I have also augmented my computer proficiency in a wide range of systems with my own home computer.

Finally, clients get the benefit of my experience, which is broad and unique. Having been a Local Sales Manager, sold nationally, and worked for a major station group, I have sold a wide variety of products in a wide variety of marketplaces. I mentioned when we talked that this exposure has broadened my outlook. It enables me to help my clients target audiences more effectively by identifying appropriate vehicles on my station or through a combination of stations (or cable systems!) -- and thus, to improve the clients' efficiencies and our bottom line.

A cliché perhaps, but one I subscribe to, is that the key to success is to "work harder and be smarter" -- both of which I want to do for you!

Sincerely,

Dierdre L. Salman
(555) 456-7890 office

After meeting with the Director of Sales and the Sales Manager several times, this jobhunter wrote to both people to make something happen. Notice the link between this letter and the previous one.

Ms. Carol Keller
Sales Manager
Cable Information Systems, Inc.
400 Avenue of the Americas
New York, NY 09876

Dear Carol:

I've enclosed a copy of a letter I sent to Anton Revinsky yesterday, which I want to make sure you see as well.

As I wrote to him, our meeting last week left me <u>more</u> convinced of the advantages I can offer Cable Information Systems -- and I wanted to reinforce these important benefits.

I am extremely eager to work with you, with CIS, and in an environment where my talents can be applied to produce <u>groundbreaking</u> bottom line results. Please let me know if there is anything else I can do to make this happen -- or if you or Anton have any further questions or need additional information or references.

I hope all is well with you and look forward to seeing you soon.

Sincerely,

Dierdre L. Salman
(555) 456-7890 office

Mr. Nicholas Thomas
Business Editor   RE: Your 6/23/9X
The Montague Corporation   *City Times* ad for
1835 Athens Boulevard   Editor/Writer
Oklahoma City, OK 09876

Dear Mr. Thomas:

I have already faxed my resumé to you but thought this packet of writing samples, written for *The Business Journal,* would be useful.

Your ad calls for a candidate experienced in developing complex subjects in-depth. As my resumé depicts, I have years of experience in interpreting, organizing, and expounding the main points of a story or an issue. In addition, I am skilled at ghost writing, which is handy for composing speeches, brochures, letters, and research reports. In the *Journal*'s "Insights" column, I translate the off-the-cuff thoughts of business leaders into logical English. Examples of this are enclosed.

Since our meeting last month, I completed a short-term project working as editor and advocate for a foreign-born doctoral candidate. I framed his ideas into clear prose, and often clarifyed conceptual problems relating to his thesis.

I sincerely hope to hear from you soon.

Cordially,

Fred Liston

Your Make Something Happen Letter can take unusual forms, as in this example.

After her interview and after sending her follow-up letters, this executive knew she was among the finalists for a job she very much wanted. To pivot the hiring decision in her direction, she sent her prospective employer this gift by messenger.

In Tiffany's signature blue box with its white ribbon, she placed a walnut shell, which she had previously emptied of its fruit.

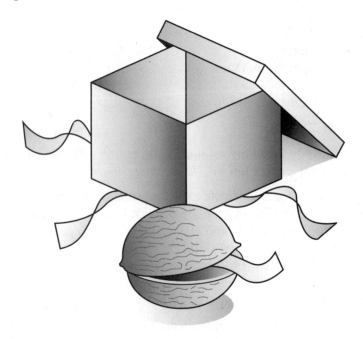

Inside the shell, she put a small slip of paper, slightly bigger than the paper on which fortunes are printed in traditional fortune cookies. Along with her handwritten signature, the paper contained the following typewritten message:

In a nutshell, I would love to work for you.

Ann Trip

She got the job.

Here is another unique take on the gutsy approach.

A jobhunter, seeking a high-level position at a leading financial services corporation, knew he was a finalist. To keep his name squarely in the mind of the decision maker, he sent an overnight express package containing a smaller box. In this box, he placed a length of adding machine tape. On the tape, he had typed the following message and signed it.

Gregory Allen

(555) 987-6543

BA, Finance

MBA, Economics

14 yrs. Experience

Published Articles

VP, Economists Society

Panelist, *Money Forum*

Exceptional Track Record

+ **Superior Recommendations**

= **Increased Profitability**
   for USD Corporation

Bottom Line: Let's make it happen!

Greg Allen

Ms. Monica Anderson, President
Anderson, Anderson & Sticht
540-87 North Cumberland Street
St. Paul, MN 09876

Dear Ms. Anderson:

With your hiring deadline fast approaching, perhaps I can simplify this difficult decision with a brief review of what I can accomplish for you.

New Business Development: Like the 40 new customers I've brought in during the last 6 months alone.

Growth: Like the 20% increase in sales I achieved last year.

Leadership: Like the respect my team members have for me as demonstrated in the letters of reference I've provided for you, and the mentoring program I created.

I have not concealed my excitement at the prospect of working with you because it's the same enthusiasm I bring to my sales efforts, and to supporting my co-workers in their efforts.

Please let me know if there is anything else I can do to influence your decision in my favor.

Sincerely,

Karen G. Kirk
(555) 765-4321 extension 43

Mr. Dominick Dunleavy
Fargo Manufacturing Corporation
1234 Main Street
Fargo, ND 09876

*Super
visual
treatment*

Dear Mr. Dunleavy:

Mediocrity
didn't take Fargo Manufacturing
to the heights it has achieved to date.

Mediocrity
won't put your bottom line at the top of the industry.

Mediocrity
is what you avoid when you hire the best.

Who is the best?

The answer is in your hands.

Sincerely,

Jorge Mirales
(555) 456-7890

Here is an effective way to handle a familiar, frustrating scenario.

Mr. Bill Coombs
Vice President, Domestic Operations
Ladimor Worldwide Enterprises
1800 Ladimor Quadrangle
Washington DC 09876

Dear Mr. Coombs:

Since you and I are in the midst of "phone tag," I thought I would write you a quick note. It was a real pleasure meeting you several weeks ago, and discussing the exciting opportunities within Ladimor Worldwide.

You mentioned that it would make sense for me to speak with John Allen to learn more about the International Division. Given your busy schedule, I have taken the liberty of contacting him directly, and have scheduled an appointment for next week. I am looking forward to meeting him and will let you know the results of our session.

Very proactive!

Thank you again for your time.

Sincerely,

Angelique Butron
(555) 765-4321 work
(555) 456-7890 home

Here is an excellent letter from a part-time worker anxious to transform her position into a full-time one.

Ms. Carolyn Grasso
President
Grasso, Milstein & Greco
1234 Main Street
Tucson, AZ 09876

Dear Ms. Grasso:

Working with you and your exceptional team over the past 16 months has been exceedingly rewarding, and for this I thank you.

My status as a consultant notwithstanding, you and your colleagues have welcomed me as a regular, valuable member of your team. You have given me the authority to supervise co-workers, create budgets, and represent the objectives of senior management in the successful execution of projects of my own design.

I am gratified to report that my efforts have produced authentic results: 52 new clients, $3.2 million in new sales, 9% reduction in overhead expenses. With the acquisition of such significant new business, the corporate culture is simultaneously rejuvenated and the corporate image is reaffirmed.

She makes it hard to argue with success.

Results such as these are precisely what I intended to achieve for you -- and what I hope to continue bringing to the firm. I would welcome the opportunity to make my success a permanent contribution at Grasso, Milstein & Greco.

Let's get together to discuss this promising partnership. I'll call you shortly.

Sincerely,

Emily Richardson
Extension 903

Mr. George J. Johnson
The Syntex Corporation
1201 Encenada Drive
Fullerton, CA 09876

Dear Mr. Johnson:

Three weeks ago, we had the opportunity to meet and discuss the possibility of providing additional office support for your agents.

Since you were just beginning to explore this prospect at that time, I realize it may be a while before you are ready to make a decision. For this reason, I am writing to restate my interest and to recap my qualifications.

My present position was a start-up position -- one that was also new to the company. In this role, I began by immediately assessing tasks that needed to be fulfilled. I then created the position and my role to most effectively meet the goals of the individual representatives, and the corporation as a whole. This required initiative, the ability to organize people and tasks, as well as the confidence to work in a new environment and quickly achieve rapport with the executives and staff.

<u>I can do the same for you.</u>

I am excited by the challenge of creating a new position. Allow me to use my expertise to make this position a meaningful, productive part of your organization.

I am available to meet again to answer any additional questions you may have.

Sincerely,

Susan Carroll
(555) 456-7890

Dr. Joan Silverstein, Chairperson
CSE-43
76-43 Queens Boulevard
Queens, NY 09876

Dear Dr. Silverstein:

I am extremely honored to be among the finalists for the position of Assistant Chairperson in District 43. Our meetings have convinced me that it would be a genuine pleasure to work with you as well as the members of your staff.

To assist you with what may be a difficult selection process, let me summarize the expertise I have acquired during my 18-year career in Special Education:

-Diagnostic and prescriptive evaluations

-Case management

-Team facilitation

-Development of IEPs and individualized curricula

-Mainstreaming

-Staff training

-Parent counseling

-Child advocacy

-Coordination of therapeutic ancillary services

-Preparation of proposals for federal, state, and private grants

I gained this diverse experience working with mentally retarded, emotionally handicapped, and multiply handicapped children from preschool age to age 21.

It would be a pleasure to bring to CSE-43 my familiarity and hands-on contributions in each of these vital areas. If there is any other information you require, please let me know. I would be happy to return for additional interviews at any time.

Thank you again for your time and consideration.

Sincerely,

Helen Cavinaw Holtswoman

Mr. Maurice Sachs
Principal, South Helena School District
One Municipal Way
South Helena, MA 09876

Dear Maurice:

Since you've seen my <u>curriculum vitae</u>, you know that I have been an educator for over 17 years.

Since we've met several times, you know that I still retain the drive, energy, and commitment it takes to excite students in a subject they find dull, at best -- irrelevant, at worst.

Since we've discussed my fortune in receiving the State of Connecticut's "Outstanding Educator Award" in 1987, 1991, and 1994, you know that my abilities are well recognized, for which I am grateful.

So, if there is any uncertainty at all, please be assured **beyond a shadow of a doubt** that I am extremely eager to bring my talents and experience to bear on behalf of the students, families, faculty, and administration of my new home in South Helena.

Thank you once again, Maurice, for your time and candor.

Most Sincerely,

Adam Rodman
(555) 456-7890 home

"Parallel construction" adds strength to the writer's message

234

Ms. Amy Finkle-Rice
Vice President
American Home Services, Inc.
4500 Lake Shore Drive
Chicago, IL 09876

Dear Ms. Finkle-Rice:

You have been so generous with your time and attention during the past few weeks, I must express my gratitude.

Rarely have I enjoyed an interview process as thoroughly as I have yours. You and your staff have made me feel entirely welcome at American Home Services. There is no doubt in my mind that I will be able to fit into your organization and corporate culture at once -- and begin contributing immediately to your reputation for service and your overall profitability.

If there is anything else I can do to demonstrate how ideal the match is between your needs and my strengths, please let me know. The opportunity to work closely with you is tremendously exciting.

Thanks again for your time and consideration.

With best regards,

Mary Anne Engstrom
(555) 765-4321 home
(555) 456-6789 work

Mr. Reginald K. Linder
President and Chief Executive Officer
The Linder Organization
7600 Corporate Drive
New Hope City, LA 09876

Dear Reg:

30% reduction in overhead. 43% reduction in operating costs. 12% reduction in staff. 20% reduction in employee benefits expenses.

Killer opening

These are the savings I achieved for Morgan Engineering and the potential I offer to The Linder Organization.

Another day (without me) … another dollar (spent).

Killer close

Sincerely,

Milton V. Childress

Chapter 8

Additional Jobhunting Letters

Effective networking pays off not only in your current job search, but in any you may undertake in the future, as well. For this reason, it's imperative that you treat with respect anyone with whom you have had contact during the jobhunt. You never know who may provide your next lead or job offer! So it pays to take a few minutes to acknowledge your interaction with those you encounter. If not, you can certainly predict who will *not* provide your next lead or job offer!

- **The Reference Request:** Always get permission to use someone as a reference. In many cases, this may be done by telephone. But when you choose to write, make your letter straightforward and to the point. Supply the person who will be serving as your reference with information on anyone who might be contacting him or her to discuss your qualifications. If you know who will be contacting your reference, say so; provide names, titles, companies, and state the position for which you are interviewing. If you can't be specific, describe the *types* of positions for which you'll be interviewing. Always send a copy of your resumé to the person serving as your reference—either with your request or afterwards. You'll find sample Reference Request Letters later in this chapter.

- **The Meeting Confirmation:** On rare occasions you may wish to confirm a meeting or an interview in writing. Such letters are always short, polite, and to the point. Reconfirm all pertinent details: date, time, location, with whom you'll be meeting, what you'll bring, what they'll bring, for what position you're interviewing, etc. By all means, reconfirm your interest in the position or the company by making your letter sound enthusiastic! Samples follow.

    (Note: If you're using your confirmation as an excuse to make a premeeting sales pitch to your interviewer or to provide additional information prior to a second meeting, you're really writing a Letter of Introduction or a Follow-up Letter; refer to the chapters that focus on these letters.)

- **The Job Acceptance:** If you choose to write one, your Acceptance Letter should be short, precise, and to the point. In it, you can simply say "yes" to a job offer. Or you can confirm, in writing, the results of your jobhunting, interview, and negotiation efforts: the terms of your employment agreement. Remember that whatever you put in writing stays on the record. So be certain your facts are accurate.

- **The Negotiation of an Offer:** Typically, negotiating a job offer is handled in person or by phone, and often by a recruiter or placement agent. If you find you must negotiate in writing, be clear and to the point. Justify your requests with support points that are important to the reader. Above all, remember that whatever you put in writing is on the record forever. Don't exaggerate, prefabricate, or make promises you can't keep.

- **The Offer Rejection:** Whether or not you've turned down a job offer in person, you may wish to put it in writing as well. You may, for example, be asked to put your rejection in writing for the company's records, or you may wish to do so for your own records. (If, however, you're writing to maintain friendly relations so that you may be considered for future positions, this is a Follow-up Letter.)

    If the interview process was lengthy, you may wish to give a reason for your decision. ("Although you had … I chose to …") Generally, there's no need to say where you've accepted an alternate job, especially if you've moved to a new field. If the person you're writing has gone out of his or her way on your behalf, be sure to acknowledge this kindness.

THE LETTER OF RESIGNATION

Congratulations! Your hard work paid off with a job offer that you've accepted. Now comes the fun part: quitting your old one!

You've heard the advice of the experts, "Don't burn your bridges." They counsel against composing a scathing, biting attack on your old boss, your mean spirited co-workers, the associate who sabotaged you, and the negative corporate culture. And they're right because you never know where these people will land when they switch jobs—perhaps at the firm you've longed to work for all your life. Who knows? You might be asked to return and serve as their boss one day! (Isn't revenge sweet?)

So now is the time to write a professional, positive letter of resignation. You simply state that you are relinquishing your position and when. That is all you are required to do, although few people stop at that. The following sample letters demonstrate several alternative methods for resigning: the happy camper, the disgruntled (but professional employee), and the one who "plays it close to the vest."

Choose your own style—just remember, whatever you put on paper remains on the record forever!

This jobhunter maintained the pleasant tone of voice she used in this letter in her subsequent Thank-You Letter (which you'll find in Chap. 6) to Professor Price.

Professor James Price
Economics Department
State University
University City, MO 09876

Dear Professor Price:

After all you've done for me -- as professor, advisor and friend -- do I dare ask for more? Well, I must, so here it goes. Would you be willing to serve as a reference for me in my job search?

As you know, I'd like to join the training program of a financial services organization in the St. Louis area. In fact, I have already interviewed with three firms, each of which has asked me to provide references. With your permission, I will have the following people contact you:

1. John Brunswick, Loan Officer
   St. Louis Federal Bank

2. Muriel Howard, Vice President
   Credit Services
   Clayton Bank and Trust

3. Leslie Rubin, President
   South County Credit Union

Knowing how busy your schedule is this time of year, I shall call your office next Wednesday during the late afternoon to see whether you're able to speak with these people.

I thank you in advance for your time and help.

Fondly,

Jennifer Lawrence

Mr. Ronald H. Burke
President
Burke Enterprises
245 East 42 Street
New York, NY 09876

Dear Ron:

I hope this letter finds you well and prosperous. During my 1990-1993 tenure at Burke Enterprises, your insistence on premier product innovations was legendary. Since then, I have kept abreast of Burke's impressive growth so I know that your admonitions are still being heeded.

As you may recall, I left Burke when my wife's firm sent her to California to open a West Coast division. After two years with the government, I am now in the process of continuing my career in product development, and would consider it an honor to add your name to the top of my list of references.

With your approval, I will authorize representatives of firms with which I am in the final stages of the selection process to contact you. I have enclosed an updated resumé with this letter to remind you of my qualifications -- and I will call you shortly to see whether you might be willing to assist me. If so, I will provide you, *in advance,* with the names of those who may be in touch with you.

Ron, I was grateful for your thoughtfulness and support when I was part of the Burke team, and I am equally grateful now for your help.

All best,

Stuart Goodman
(555) 456-7890 home

Ms. Loretta Smits
Personnel Officer
HealthCom, Inc.
340 Woodside Drive
Pleasantville, NY 09876

Dear Ms. Smits:

I am looking forward to meeting you on January 12, 199X at 3:00 p.m. at the Pleasantville Hyatt to discuss the Programming position in your Eastern Division.

I feel certain that my training and practical experience will prove valuable to you, and I am eager to provide you with details on my background.

Until then I am sincerely,

Alfred Strong
(555) 456-7890

Ms. Loretta Smits
Personnel Officer
HealthCom, Inc.
340 Woodside Drive
Pleasantville, NY 09876

Dear Ms. Smits:

It is with great pleasure that I accept your offer to serve as a Programmer for your Eastern Division. I look forward to joining HealthCom beginning on March 1, 199X with a starting salary of $35,000 per year.

I am especially eager to work with Dawn Sinclair in her new Urban Development Unit.

Thank you for your assistance and consideration.

Most sincerely,

Carol L. Zimmer

This letter and the one that follows differ only slightly—but on the rare occasions that job negotiations are put in writing, details like these are of key importance.

Mr. Harold C. Pynter
American Eagle Publishers
1200 Wacker Drive
Chicago, IL 09876

Dear Harold:

You've certainly built an exceptional editorial team over the years, and your offer to join it is enormously gratifying.

As you know, I am very eager to accept this honor. I look forward to bringing my contacts, authors, and their projects in progress to American Eagle. Because these relationships are ones I've nurtured for more than 10 years, they're naturally of great value to me -- and to you. The profit potential they represent is substantial. I feel it is reasonable and fair to adhere to my request for a 10% stake in the profits these properties generate.

Harold, in light of the many benefits of our joining forces, this detail seems minor. It is, however, of great importance to me. Let's agree on this right away, and launch our promising partnership!

I look forward to hearing from you.

Sincerely,

Jim Enright

Mr. Harold C. Pynter
American Eagle Publishers
1200 Wacker Drive
Chicago, IL 09876

Dear Harold:

You've certainly built an exceptional editorial team over the years, and your offer to join it is enormously gratifying.

As you know, I am very eager to accept this honor. I look forward to bringing my contacts, authors, and their projects in progress to American Eagle. Because these relationships are ones I've nurtured for more than 10 years, they're naturally of great value to me -- and to you. The profit potential they represent is substantial. I feel it is reasonable to request a share in the profits these properties generate.

Let's agree on a specific percentage right away, and launch our promising partnership!

I look forward to hearing from you.

Sincerely,

Jim Enright

Ms. Loretta Smits
Personnel Officer
HealthCom, Inc.
340 Woodside Drive
Pleasantville, NY 09876

Dear Ms. Smits:

Thank you very much for offering me the position of Programmer for your Eastern Division. Unfortunately, because I have just accepted another firm's offer, I am unable to join HealthCom's staff at this time.

I am very grateful to you for your assistance during the interview process, and I thank you for your consideration.

Sincerely,

Charlotte Milman-Speers

Mr. Anthony Rubens
Personnel Officer
Johnson & Miller, Inc.
6500 Executive Parkway
Bristol, PA 09876

Dear Mr. Rubens:

I am writing to withdraw my name from consideration for the position of Executive Administrative Assistant with your firm as I have accepted an offer from another company.

However, I must thank you for your time and candor in describing both the position and the corporate culture. You were most kind, and I appreciate the encouragement you offered me.

With best wishes for your continued success, I am

Crystal E. Evans

This letter is short, sweet, and to the point—very professional!

May 15, 199X

Ms. Claire Danielle, Vice President
Burger Products International
67676 Walton Way
Nanaimo, AK 09876

Dear Ms. Danielle:

With this letter, I hereby submit my resignation from Burger Products International, effective Friday June 4, 199X, to further my career in Facilities Management.

At your convenience, I will be glad to discuss the reassignment of my work to others.

I wish you good luck and continued success.

Sincerely,

Matthew Lewis

This writer reminds her boss of the productive changes she's implemented. Nice touch!

February 15, 199X

Mr. William Hedger, President
The Technix Corporation
9755 Old Lyme Road
Old Lyme CT 09876

Dear Mr. Hedger:

I am writing to inform you that I will be resigning my responsibilities as Comptroller effective March 1, 199X.

I realize that selecting and introducing a new Comptroller may be difficult, and I will do whatever I can to make this transition a smooth one. In large part, the streamlined accounting and recordkeeping practices I developed during the last 4 years will help a new Comptroller master our systems and data quickly.

I am pleased to have had the opportunity to work with Technix. I wish you continued success and growth.

Sincerely,

Christine Mikabi

The cleverly worded opening paragraph may leave Mr. Andrews wondering what this writer's opinion of the company really is—but its clever wording won't endanger the writer's reputation or future.

November 3, 199X

Mr. Jack Andrews
Andrews Housewares
189 East 40th Street
Quincy, IL 09876

Dear Jack:

Effective November 30, I am resigning from my job as Media Director at Mercury Advertising. My decision to leave is both personal and professional, and does not reflect a change in my opinion of the company.

Donna Frey has performed admirably as my assistant, and is well equipped to assume my responsibilities at once. If you prefer to look outside the company to replace me, I will be happy to assist in the search between now and the end of the month.

Thank you for your continued confidence in me throughout the past two years.

Sincerely,

Thomas Keith

Chapter 9

Killer Resources

If you've made it this far, the hard part is done. You've identified your strengths, determined what benefits they offer your next employer, and fashioned them into sentences and paragraphs you can use in your jobhunting letters. You've written attention-grabbing openings, action-oriented closings. You're ready to mail your own killer cover letters. Before you seal those envelopes, take a few minutes to be certain that you've thought of everything.

The following pages will help ensure that your letters are really as strong as they possibly can be.

First, scan the list of words and phrases to avoid. If your letter is replete with jargon, your message may not get through as clearly as it should.

Then, run down the Cover Letter Checklist, comparing it to your letters. The Checklist will help ensure you've "covered all your bases," "have all your ducks in a row," and are, indeed, ready to mail your Killer Cover Letters.

*The most valuable of all talents
is that of never using two words
when one will do.*

—Thomas Jefferson

WORDS AND PHRASE TO AVOID

AVOID	USE INSTEAD
additionally	in addition
along the lines of	like
alright	all right
alot	a lot
answer in the affirmative	yes
arrived at the conclusion that	concluded
as per	I find _or_ according to
as stated above	from these facts _or_ as I have shown
at a later date	later
at the present writing	now
at the present time	now
at the time of three in the afternoon	at 3:00 p.m.
at this point in time	now
attached hereto	attached
attached herein	attached
attached please find	attached is _or_ attached you'll find _or_ I enclose
awaiting the favor of a response	please let me know
beg to inform you	inform you
came at a time when	came when
city of New Orleans	New Orleans
close to the point of	close to
concerning the matter of	concerning _or_ about
due to the fact that	because
enclosed herewith	enclosed
enclosed please find	enclosed is _or_ enclosed you'll find _or_ I enclose
fewer in number	fewer, less
file away	file
for the purpose	for _or_ to
for the reason that	because
for your information	(delete entirely)
in accordance with your request	as you requested,
in the amount of	for
in respect to the matter of	about _or_ regarding
in the area of	about
in the field of accounting	in accounting
in the near future	soon _or_ shortly
in the neighborhood of	about
in this day and age	now _or_ today
in as much as	since
irregardless	regardless
is at this time	is
most unique	unique

my personal opinion	my opinion
myriad of	myriad
of the fact that	(delete entirely)
on the grounds that	because
on the occasion of	when (or state occasion)
prior to	before
prolong the duration	prolong
quality	high quality or low quality, superior quality or poor quality
shows a preference for	prefers
subsequent to	after
that is the reason why	that is why
the reason is due to	because
the undersigned	I
under separate cover	(delete entirely; say how it's being sent: by airmail, fax, etc.)
utilize	use
with reference to	about
with regard to	about or regarding
with respect to	about
without further delay	now or immediately

COVER LETTER CHECKLIST

_____ Have you used the same type of paper for your resumé, letter, and envelope?

_____ Do your name, address, and phone number(s) appear at the top of each page?

_____ Have you verified that you are addressing the company by its correct name (Reebok International Ltd., *not* Reebok, Inc.)

_____ Is your envelope typed, not handwritten?

_____ Have you signed your letter?

_____ Have you proofread your letter before *and after* using your computer's spelling check function? (Remember: Your computer won't catch an error such as "thin" instead of "this.")

_____ Does your letter look visually appealing?

_____ If your letter is skimmed, will your reader be impressed with key points?

_____ Will your reader know to which advertisement you're responding? In which position you're interested?

_____ Will your opening make the reader want to read on?

_____ Does the body of your letter support your opening?

_____ Is your letter honest?

_____ Is your tone of voice conversational, not stuffy?

_____ Have you avoided repeating, word-for-word, many of the details that appear on your resumé?

_____ Have you summarized your experience and education?

_____ Have you described your strengths from your reader's point of view? ("What this means for you is …")

_____ Did you provide necessary background information in cases where a reader or recruiter is unfamiliar with you or your area of speciality?

_____ Have you used any terminology that might be unfamiliar to your reader? Can you simplify it? If not, have you defined it clearly?

_____ Have you told your reader what you will do to follow up?

_____ Did you supply any and all information your reader will need to contact you or comply with your request for help?

Index of Letters
That Address Specific Issues

Many of the letters in this book and on the accompanying disk address specific issues of concern in today's jobhunting environment. To help you locate ways in which you might handle such situations, many of the letters throughout the book are labeled according to the issue they address. Such letters are also listed below for quick reference.

For example, if you are returning to work after an absence, check the letters listed under "Workforce Return." If you are switching fields, refer to the letters listed under "Career Change." Graduating seniors and recent MBAs, be sure to review those listed below under "Student" for ideas to adapt and use in your own letters.

ISSUE	CHAPTER—LETTER NUMBER
Career Change	3-3, 3-6, 3-7, 4-20, 4-26, 4-37, 4-59, 4-71, 4-87, 4-88, 4-89, 4-111, 4-114
Confidentiality	4-49, 4-52, 4-58, 4-76, 4-92, 4-116
Create an Opportunity	4-110, 7-16
International	4-61, 6-4
Language Abilities	4-10, 4-23, 4-25, 4-61, 4-65, 4-70, 4-98, 4-117
Layoffs/Hiring Freeze/Downsizing	3-1, 3-7, 3-8, 3-10, 4-8, 4-46, 4-64, 4-120, 5-17
Multiple Jobs	4-11, 4-46
Part-Time/Full-Time/Freelance	3-10, 4-21, 4-72, 4-90, 4-102, 4-110, 7-15
Phone Tag	7-14
Relocation	3-4, 4-22, 4-61, 4-68, 4-90, 4-120
Salary Discussion 4-63,	2-2, 4-1, 4-11, 4-25, 4-32, 4-34, 4-42, 4-53, 4-56, 4-60, 4-75, 4-98, 4-121
Student	3-14, 3-16, 4-9, 4-12, 4-13, 4-14, 4-15, 4-16, 4-17, 4-19, 4-25, 4-26, 4-54, 4-61, 4-88, 4-90, 4-94, 6-6, 6-7, 8-1
Workforce Return	2-3, 3-4, 4-47, 4-89, 4-91, 4-93, 4-95
Writing to Recruiter	4-10, 4-20, 4-39, 4-44, 4-79, 4-118

Index of Letters by Industry and Job Title

All the letters in this book and on the accompanying disk are listed below by industry. Jobs that fall under more than one category are listed under each grouping that may apply. For example, an Insurance Sales cover letter is listed under both "Financial Services" and "Sales."

Most importantly, don't limit yourself by reading only letters dealing with a specific job. Take the time to skim many of the letters in this book. Since your letters should not repeat what's on your resumé, cover letters written by jobhunters in fields unrelated to your own will contain ideas that you can easily adapt for use in your own letters.

INDUSTRY/JOB TITLE	CHAPTER—LETTER NUMBER
Administration	*See* Business—General, Senior Management
Advertising/Marketing/Public Relations	
Art Director	4-30
Assistant Advertising Manager	4-38
Copywriter	4-31
Design	3-11
Director, Corporate Marketing	4-33
Events Planner	4-28
Market Research	4-39
Marketing Associate	4-118, 6-1
Marketing Communications Supervisor	4-1
Marketing Planner	4-32
Marketing Manager	1-4
Marketing Representative/Sales	4-41
Product Management	4-40
Public Relations	3-10
Public Relations Manager	4-29
Senior Marketing Associate	4-43, 4-44
Architecture	
Senior Architect	4-68
Arts	
Actor	4-80, 4-81, 4-82, 4-83
Film Project Coordinator	4-86
General Networking	3-6, 3-7
Producer	4-84
Teaching Artist	4-85, 5-15
Model/Actor	5-10
Business—General	
Administrative Assistant	4-23, 4-89
Accounts Receivable Coordinator	4-53
Bookkeeper	5-13
Director, Human Resources and Administration	4-111

Director, Quality Management	4-112
Director, Productivity Improvement	4-113
Executive Secretary	4-24, 4-117
Office Administrator	4-25
Market Research	4-38
Marketing Manager	1-4
Product Manager	4-35, 4-39
Product Development	4-36, 4-37
Senior Subcontracts Administrator	4-52

Computers

Communications Specialist	4-77
Data Processing—General	3-3
General Follow-Up	5-17
MIS Manager	4-75
Network Administrator	4-76, 4-119
Program Design	4-74
Senior Executive	4-78
Word Processor	4-69, 4-70, 4-71
Word Processing Format Specialist	4-72

Construction/Building Management

Building Superintendent	4-65
Construction	4-64
Facilities Management	5-7

Education

Director, Human Resources and Administration	4-111
Director of Development (Fund Raising)	4-114
English Teacher	4-90
Kindergarten Teacher	4-88
Special Education	7-17
Speech Pathologist	4-94
Teacher	4-87, 7-2, 7-18

Electronics

General	3-1
Telecommunications: Assistant Advertising Manager	4-33
Telephone Repair	2-2
Senior National Sales Representative	4-42
Systems Technician	4-73

Engineering

Electrical Engineer	4-79
Environmental Engineering	4-61
Training Engineer	4-108

Entry Level

General from Student	4-9, 4-12, 4-13, 4-14, 4-15, 4-16, 4-17, 4-18, 4-20, 4-21
Paralegal	4-20, 4-21

Financial Services

Agricultural Economist	3-2
Cash Management Sales Officer	4-56
Customer Service Representative	2-1
Electronics Funds Transfer	3-5
Financial Analyst	4-54
Financial Planning	1-2
Insurance Sales	5-1
Investment Broker	4-55
Investments—General	3-8

Lending Officer	4-58
Operations Manager	5-2
Private Banker	4-57
Sales	3-9
Senior Lender	4-59
Senior Executive	7-11
Training Program	4-18, 8-1

Health Care/Medical

Child Care Worker	4-91
Dental Hygienist	4-92
Director, Quality Improvement	4-96
EMS, Assistant Director	4-98
Medical Research and Design	5-4
Nurse	3-4, 4-95
Personal Trainer	4-99
Pharmaceuticals Technical Writer	5-16
Senior Pharmacist	4-97
Speech Pathologist	4-94
X-Ray Technician	2-4

Hospitality   *See* Service/Travel/Hospitality

Human Resources/Training

Corporate Trainer	4-107
Director, Human Resources	4-111
Employee Benefits Manager	4-106
Management and Quality Training	4-109
On-Staff Recruiter	4-110
Training	3-17
Training Engineer	4-108

Law

Attorney	5-3
Entry-Level Paralegal	4-20, 4-21
Paralegal	4-22

Management Consulting

Consulting Associate	4-26
Director, Quality Management	4-112
Director, Productivity Improvement	4-113
General	7-15
General Consulting	4-27

Marketing   *See* Advertising/Marketing/Public Relations, Sales

Medical   *See* Health Care/Medical

Public Relations   *See* Advertising/Marketing/Public Relations

Publishing

Editor	8-5, 8-6
Editor/Writer	7-9
Editorial Assistant	4-105
Technical Writer	5-16

Real Estate

Real Estate—General	4-66
Real Estate Planner	4-67

Restaurant   *See* Service/Travel/Hospitality

Retail

Assistant Buyer	5-14
Director Retail Operations	4-50

Distribution Manager	4-51
Retail Sales	4-47, 4-48
Senior Buyer	4-49

Sales

Account Executive	4-34, 7-1
Advertising Space Sales	4-46
Broadcast Sales Representative	7-7, 7-8
Cash Management Sales Officer	4-56
Corporate Travel Sales Representative	7-6
Cruise Product Development	4-37
Entry Level	4-15
Financial	3-9
General	4-121, 5-5, 5-6, 7-12, 7-15
Insurance	5-1
Product Manager	4-35
Marketing Representative	4-40
National Sales Representative	4-42
Sales Manager	7-4, 7-5
Telemarketing	3-12, 4-45

Security

Noise Abatement Officer	4-101
Security Officer	4-62, 4-63
Senior Security Management	5-9

Senior Management

Chief Financial Officer	4-115. 4-116
Computer Communications	4-78
General	4-120
Director, Management and Quality Training	4-109
Director, Human Resources and Administration	4-111
Director, Quality Management	4-112
Director, Productivity Improvement	4-113
Director of Development	4-114
Research Director	4-60
Security	5-9

Service/Travel/Hospitality

Casual Van Driver	4-102
Chauffeur	4-104
Corporate Travel Sales Representative	7-6
Cruise Product Development	4-37
Customer Service Representative	4-19
Esthetician	4-100
General/Language Skills	4-10
Personal Trainer	4-99
Restaurant Manager	3-18
Travel Agent	2-3
Wine Specialist	4-103

Student   *See* Entry Level in this index and Student in Issues index

Social Services

Child Care Worker	4-91
Social Worker	4-93

Theatre   *See* Arts

Training   *See* Human Resources/Training

Travel   *See* Service/Travel/Hospitality

About the Authors

Sandra Podesta is a principal in the DeMartino Marketing Group with 20 years' experience as an advertising copywriter for *Fortune* 500 corporations and advertising agencies. **Andrea Paxton** is a recruiter who has worked extensively with every phase of the interview, selection, and hiring process for such corporations as Chase Manhattan Bank and John Hancock Financial Services. This book is a product of their successful seminar on writing for the job search.